CHILD CARE
and EDUCATION

NVQ/SVQ LEVEL 3 WORKBOOK

Teena Jennings, Kathryn Ward, Dawn Smith,
Audrey Farley and Marilyn Bradburn

Hodder & Stoughton

A MEMBER OF THE HODDER HEADLINE GROUP

British Library Cataloguing in Publication Data

A catalogue entry for this title is available from the British Library

ISBN 0 340 64334 X

First published 1996
Impression number   10   9   8   7   6   5   4   3   2   1
Year   2000   1999   1998   1997   1996

Typeset by Wearset, Boldon, Tyne and Wear.
Printed in Great Britain for Hodder & Stoughton Educational, a division of Hodder Headline Plc, 338 Euston Road, London NW1 3BH by The Bath Press, Bath

CONTENTS

ACKNOWLEDGEMENTS

The authors would like to thank the Birmingham College of Food, Tourism and Creative Studies for providing the resources and administrative support needed to complete this project.

We would also like to thank Sarah Marlow for her secretarial support, Ben Cunningham, Jacqueline Gallagher, Joan Hendy, Frances Pegg, Pamela Steer and the Divisional Manager, Kate Garret, for their advice and good humour during this project.

INTRODUCTION

The *NVQ/SVQ Child Care and Education Level 3 Workbook* is divided into 22 units.

Generic units

The first four units are generic and if you have successfully completed Level 2 Child Care and Education you do not need to repeat them.

These units are:

C.2   Care for children's physical needs
E.1   Maintain a child orientated environment
E.2   Maintain the safety of children
P.2   Establish and maintain relationships with parents of young children

Core units

The next seven units must also be completed to achieve the NVQ Level 3 Child Care and Education.

These units are:

C.3   Promote the physical development of young children
C.5   Promote children's social and emotional development
C.7   Provide for the management of children's behaviour
C.10   Promote children's sensory and intellectual development
C.11   Promote the development of children's language and communication skills
C.15   Contribute to the protection of children from abuse
C.16   Observe and assess the development and behaviour of children

Note: If you have successfully completed Level 2 Child Care and Education you need only complete Element 6 of Unit C.5 (pages 79–82) and Element 4 of Unit C.7 (pages 97–101).

Endorsements

You will also need to complete a group of units related to *one* of the following endorsements:

Endorsement A   Group Care and Education

C.14   Care for and promote the development of babies
M.4   Work with colleagues in a team
M.7   Plan, implement and evaluate activities and experiences to promote children's learning and development
M.8   Plan, implement and evaluate routines for young children

Endorsement B   Family Day Care

C.14   Care for and promote the development of babies
P.8   Establish and maintain arrangements with parents for the provision of a child care service
M.2   Carry out the administration of the provision for care/education setting
M.8   Plan, implement and evaluate routines for young children

Endorsement C   Pre-School Provision

P.3   Involve parents in play and other learning activities with young children
P.5   Involve parents in a group for young children
M.4   Work with colleagues in a team
M.7   Plan, implement and evaluate activities and experiences to promote children's learning and development

Endorsement D   Childcare and Education (Special Needs)

C.17   Contribute to the care and education of children with special needs
C.18   Develop a structured programme for a child in partnership with parents
M.6   Work with other professionals

GUIDE TO WORKBOOK

- It will be necessary to write your answers to the workbook tasks on numbered sheets in a loose-leaf file; you should use the space below each task to record the relevant page number from the file.
- You can monitor your progress using the checklist provided at the beginning of each unit.
- Remember confidentiality at all times when completing tasks from the workbook and portfolio activities, for example, do not use names of the settings; do not use surnames and, if necessary, change first names so that individuals cannot be identified.
- A glossary of key terms is provided at the end of the workbook.

GUIDE TO PORTFOLIO ACTIVITIES

- You should organise the portfolio activities in a separate file and cross-reference them to the activities in the workbook using the unit wide and/or knowledge evidence criteria.
- One activity may be used as evidence for a number of different criteria.
- You will find guidance on setting out individual portfolio activities throughout the workbook.

C.2 CARE FOR CHILDREN'S PHYSICAL NEEDS
UNIT WIDE KNOWLEDGE

	Criteria	Unit wide knowledge	Date completed
PROGRESS CHECKLIST	C.2.a	Basic knowledge of children's development 6 weeks to 8 years and how provision for their physical needs affects their development.	
	C.2.b	The development and recognition of socially accepted behaviour and ability to understand and comply with socially accepted norms.	
	C.2.c	Variation in cultural and religious practices and customs and their implications for caring for children's physical needs.	
	C.2.d	Stereotypical assumptions in assessing and providing for children's physical needs and how to avoid/challenge them.	
	C.2.e	Health and safety requirements relevant to the setting and how to obtain further advice.	
	C.2.f	Methods and techniques for communicating with children and adults including verbal and non-verbal communication.	
	C.2.g	The boundaries of confidentiality for the setting and how, when and to whom information can be passed.	

USEFUL BOOKS

Babies and Young Children Book 1 – Development 0–7. Beaver *et al.* (1994) Stanley Thornes.
Caring for the Under 8s. Jennie and Lance Linden (1993) Macmillan.
From Birth to Five Years. Mary Sheridan (1987) NFER Nelson.
Child Care and Development. Pamela Minett (1985) John Murray.

✓ Grid C.2

Please tick box when activity is complete.
P = *Portfolio Activity*

C.2.a

C.2.1.a	C.2.1.b	C.2.1.c	C.2.4.a	C.2.4.b	C.2.4.c
P		P	P	P	P
C.2.4.d	C.2.4.e	C.2.4.f	C.2.1.i	C.2.1.j	C.2.5.a
P	P	P			P
C.2.5.b	C.2.5.c	C.2.5.d	C.2.5.e	C.2.5.f	C.2.5.g

C.2.b

C.2.2.f
P

C.2.c

C.2.1.e	C.2.1.f	C.2.1.g	C.2.4.h

C.2.d

C.2.2.e

C.2.f

C.2.3.j	C.2.3.k	C.2.3.h

C.2.e

C.2.1.d	C.2.2.a	C.2.2.b	C.2.2.c	C.2.2.d	C.2.2.g	C.2.3.a
P	P	P				
C.2.3.b	C.2.3.c	C.2.3.d	C.2.3.e	C.2.3.f	C.2.3.g	C.2.3.i
		P	P	P		

C.2.g

C.2.3.1
P

PORTFOLIO ACTIVITY SUMMARY

Criteria	Portfolio page reference	0–1	1–4	4–7
C.2.a	See below and pages 5, 12 and 15 for Portfolio Activities			
C.2.b	See page 8 for Portfolio Activity			
C.2.e	See pages 5, 8, 10 and 11 for Portfolio Activities			
C.2.g	See page 11 for Portfolio Activity			

C.2 Care for children's physical needs

 ### C.2.a Portfolio Activity

Present a range of observations which demonstrate your knowledge of children's development from 6 weeks to 8 years and show the importance of taking account of this when considering safety arrangements.

There is no need to complete C.2.a if you have completed E.2.a but please provide a completion date.

C.2.b, C.2.c, C.2.d, C.2.e, C.2.f, C.2.g – see grid C.2 for cross-referenced knowledge evidence activities.

C.2.1 Provide food and drinks for children

PROGRESS CHECKLIST	Criteria	Knowledge evidence	Date completed
	C.2.1.a	The nutritional value of common foodstuffs and drinks and what constitutes a balanced diet.	
	C.2.1.b	The nutritional value in relation to size of portions and methods of preparation.	
	C.2.1.c	Ways of presenting food and drink that are attractive to children and easy to manage.	
	C.2.1.d	Health and safety requirements in relation to food preparation and storage.	
	C.2.1.e	Common dietary requirements associated with religious and cultural practices.	
	C.2.1.f	The importance of valuing and introducing to children cultural and religious variations in types of food, type of preparation and utensils and eating habits.	
	C.2.1.g	The role of food in social and cultural life and in shaping attitudes and behaviour.	
	C.2.1.h	The variety of food preferences and eating habits children may have and the way they may change over time.	
	C.2.1.i	Common food allergies and implications for diets.	
	C.2.1.j	Effects of illness and emotional disturbance on appetite.	

USEFUL BOOKS

Babies and Young Children Book 1 – Development 0–7. Beaver *et al.* (1994) Stanley Thornes.
Babies and Young Children Book 2 – Work and Care. Beaver *et al.* (1995) Stanley Thornes.

PORTFOLIO ACTIVITY SUMMARY				
Criteria	**Portfolio page reference**	**0–1**	**1–4**	**4–7**
C.2.1.a	See below for Portfolio Activity			
C.2.1.c	See below for Portfolio Activity			
C.2.1.d	See below for Portfolio Activity			

C.2.1.a Portfolio Activity

Plan a menu you would give to a three-year-old child including meals and snacks to ensure a balanced diet for a day.

C.2.1.b Why is it preferable to give children some raw fruit and vegetables?

....

Why should cakes and biscuits only be given at a special occasion?

....

C.2.1.c Portfolio Activity

Plan a dish suitable for a child's lunch and draw a diagram showing how you could present it. Include a list of foods and three reasons why it is important to present children's food attractively.

C.2.1.d Portfolio Activity

Find out the health and safety requirements in relation to food preparation and storage in your work setting.

C.2.1.e Draw up a table like the one on page 6 and tick the foods allowed
by each group.

C.2.1.i ....

C.2.1.f Why do we need to know about cultural and religious variations in food?

....

	Jewish	Sikh	Muslim	Buddhist	Hindu	Rastafarian	Christian	Free from artificial colourings	Allergic to dairy foods
Kosher									
Halal									
Beef									
Pork									
Lamb									
Chicken									
Crisps									
Ice-cream									
Cheese									
Eggs									
Oranges									
Tea/coffee									
Nuts									
Beans									
Yams									
Rice									
Milk									
Cereals									
Chapati									
Chinese mushrooms									
Bread									
Sausages									

C.2.1.g   Consider the following four ways of eating and how each may shape children's
C.2.1.h   attitudes and behaviour:

    (1) formal family meal;
    (2) family sitting around table watching television whilst eating;
    (3) children eating separately from parents;
    (4) children eating their own food to suit themselves.

    ....

C.2.1.j   List five reasons why it is important to prevent obesity in children.

    ....

C.2.2 Contribute to children's personal hygiene

	Criteria	Knowledge evidence	Date completed
PROGRESS CHECKLIST	C.2.2.a	The general health and hygiene requirements of young children and what constitutes appropriate personal hygiene routines.	
	C.2.2.b	The purpose, application and storage of toiletries, cleaning materials and equipment.	
	C.2.2.c	The causes of cross-infection and procedures to prevent cross-infection.	
	C.2.2.d	The procedures for dealing with waste products.	
	C.2.2.e	The methods of caring for the personal hygiene of young children and how these may vary with family/cultural background, skin and hair types, and across child care settings.	
	C.2.2.f	The ways in which toilet training and hygiene routines are said to shape attitudes and behaviour.	
	C.2.2.g	Signs of infection, abrasions and other abnormalities including variation from normal stools and urine and their significance.	

USEFUL BOOKS

Child Care and Development, 3rd edition. P. Minett (1985) John Murray.
Babies and Young Children Book 2 – Work and Care. Beaver *et al.* (1995) Stanley Thornes.

PORTFOLIO ACTIVITY SUMMARY				
Criteria	**Portfolio page reference**	**0–1**	**1–4**	**4–7**
C.2.2.a	See page 8 for Portfolio Activity			
C.2.2.b	See page 8 for Portfolio Activity			
C.2.2.f	See page 8 for Portfolio Activity			

C.2.2.a Portfolio Activity

Design a poster for the bathroom describing the routine you would use when supervising young children using the toilet to encourage good personal hygiene.

C.2.2.b Portfolio Activity

Select five pieces of equipment/cleaning materials. Describe the purpose, application and storage of them.

C.2.2.c   List three ways in which infection can be spread from one source to another.

....

List three ways in which the spread of infection can be prevented.

....

C.2.2.d   Describe the procedure you would use when dealing with a soiled potty.

....

C.2.2.e   Give three cultural factors which need to be taken into account when planning hygiene routines for children from different ethnic groups.

....

C.2.2.f Portfolio Activity

Design a leaflet for parents/carers to encourage positive attitudes with regard to toilet training and hygiene routines.

C.2.2.g   Why and to whom would you report the following:

(*a*) child: hot, flushed and fretful;

....

(*b*) green smelly stools;

....

(*c*) urine smelling of acetone (nail polish remover).

....

C.2.3 Respond to illness in a child

Criteria	Knowledge evidence	Date completed
C.2.3.a	Symptoms of commonly encountered illnesses and methods of dealing with them.	
C.2.3.b	The significance and criticality of symptoms in relation to age/development of children.	
C.2.3.c	Importance of keeping records of significant medical conditions and of medication administered.	
C.2.3.d	Sources of help in identification and response to symptoms.	
C.2.3.e	The legal requirements re: parental consent to administration of medicines, creams, lotions, dressings and reporting of communicable diseases.	
C.2.3.f	Procedures for dealing with a child who is unconscious.	
C.2.3.g	The recognition of symptoms in children of varying skin tones.	
C.2.3.h	Children's emotional needs when unwell and the effects of illness on subsequent behaviour.	
C.2.3.i	Storage requirements and need for proper labelling of medicines.	
C.2.3.j	Parents' emotional needs and own roles when children are unwell and the effects of illness.	
C.2.3.k	Implications of chronic medical conditions for the child's age.	
C.2.3.l	When, how and to whom to record and report incidents.	

PROGRESS CHECKLIST

USEFUL BOOKS

Child's Play – A Parent's Manual. The Diagram Group: Corgi.

PORTFOLIO ACTIVITY SUMMARY				
Criteria	**Portfolio page reference**	**0–1**	**1–4**	**4–7**
C.2.3.d	See below for Portfolio Activity			
C.2.3.e	See below for Portfolio Activity			
C.2.3.f	See page 11 for Portfolio Activity			
C.2.3.l	See page 11 for Portfolio Activity			

C.2.3.a   Name the '3 Cs' which probably account for most childhood infectious illnesses in the pre-school and early school years.

....

C.2.3.b   At what stage are children most vulnerable to infection?

....

C.2.3.c   Why is it important to keep records of medical conditions and of medicine
C.2.3.i   given?

....

What four checks need to be made before you give medicines?

....

 ### C.2.3.d *Portfolio Activity*

Where would you go to find out about a child's health and developmental progress?

 ### C.2.3.e *Portfolio Activity*

Find out the policy of your workplace with regard to parental consent to administration of medicines, creams, lotions, dressings and reporting of communicable diseases.

C.2.3.f Portfolio Activity

Outline the procedures for dealing with a child who is unconscious.

C.2.3.g   How may spots or a rash show on a child with

      (*a*) dark skin tone?

....

      (*b*) pale skin tone?

....

C.2.3.h   Why may a child have special emotional needs when unwell?

....

C.2.3.j   How might you support a parent whose child is ill?

....

C.2.3.k   How may a child's care be affected by chronic medical conditions?

....

C.2.3.l Portfolio Activity

Find out to whom you would report an accident in your workplace and how it would be recorded.

C.2.4 Provide opportunities for children to rest or sleep

PROGRESS CHECKLIST	Criteria	Knowledge evidence	Date completed
	C.2.4.a	The importance of rest/sleep or quiet periods as part of the daily routine and of matching the routines of home and child care setting.	
	C.2.4.b	The variation of rest and sleep requirements of children at different stages and as individuals.	
	C.2.4.c	How to use space and equipment to promote opportunities for rest and/or sleep.	
	C.2.4.d	Methods of managing conflict between children in choice of rest or activity.	
	C.2.4.e	The variation in approaches to informal/formal bedtimes, adapted by families of different backgrounds.	
	C.2.4.f	The problems for families when the requirements for a child's sleep/rest pattern do not match the family's evening lifestyle.	

USEFUL BOOKS

Babies and Young Children Book 2 – Work and Care. Beaver *et al.* (1995) Stanley Thornes.

PORTFOLIO ACTIVITY SUMMARY				
Criteria	Portfolio page reference	0–1	1–4	4–7
C.2.4.a–f	See below for Portfolio Activity			

 ## C.2.4.a, C.2.4.b, C.2.4.c, C.2.4.d, C.2.4.e, C.2.4.f Portfolio Activity

You are working in a family centre. How will you organise rest/sleep periods as part of the daily routine and how will you liaise with parents?

The young babies may be sleeping in cots or prams. What would you use to promote rest/sleep for older children and how would you encourage them to have a rest/sleep?

Families may differ in their approach to rest/sleep patterns. How will this affect your routine?

You are working in a family centre and a mother asks you the following. How will you answer?

> *(a) Why is sleep important?*
> *(b) Do all children need the same amount of sleep?*

C.2.5 Provide opportunities for children's exercise

	Criteria	Knowledge evidence	Date completed
PROGRESS CHECKLIST	C.2.5.a	The general role of exercise in promoting physical growth and development.	
	C.2.5.b	The importance of adequate supervision for children during physical exercise.	
	C.2.5.c	The relationship between level of child's development and physical abilities and appropriate exercise.	
	C.2.5.d	How to undertake simple adaptations to equipment and spatial arrangement of equipment to suit children's needs and safety requirements.	
	C.2.5.e	Indicators of stereotypical approaches to exercise and how to provide non-stereotypical exercise and play.	
	C.2.5.f	Methods of providing for different types of exercise and physical abilities.	
	C.2.5.g	The role of physical achievement in developing self-confidence.	

USEFUL BOOKS

Babies and Young Children Book 1 – Development 0–7. Beaver *et al.* (1994) Stanley Thornes.

PORTFOLIO ACTIVITY SUMMARY

Criteria	Portfolio page reference	0–1	1–4	4–7
C.2.5.a–g	See page 15 for Portfolio Activity			

C.2.5.a, C.2.5.b, C.2.5.c, C.2.5.d, C.2.5.e, C.2.5.f, C.2.5.g *Portfolio Activity*

You are responsible for a group of four three-year-old boys and girls. One girl is Muslim, one boy is Sikh.

Plan an exercise programme for them to last six weeks. Give reasons why an exercise programme is necessary. Say how you will ensure the children's safety.

Draw a plan of the area you will use for the exercise session. How could you adapt this for a group of six-year-olds?

Include your ideas for providing a non-stereotypical approach and discuss how your programme will help the children to develop self-confidence.

E.1 Maintain a child orientated environment

Unit wide knowledge

Criteria	Unit wide knowledge	Date completed
E.1.a	The role of the environment in children's learning and in meeting their needs.	
E.1.b	The relationship between the home environment and the care/education environment.	

(PROGRESS CHECKLIST)

Useful books

Ways to Display – A practical guide for teachers. Derek Greenstreet (1985) Ward Lock.
Special Issues in Child Care. M. O'Hagan and M. Smith (1994) Bailliere Tindall.

Grid E.1

Please tick box when activity is complete.
P = *Portfolio Activity*

E.1.a	E.1.1.a	E.1.1.b	E.1.1.c	E.1.1.d	E.1.1.e	E.1.1.f
			P	P	P	
	E.1.1.g	E.1.2.a	E.1.2.b	E.1.2.c	E.1.2.d	
				P	P	

E.1.b	E.1.3.a	E.1.3.b	E.1.3.c	E.1.3.d
			P	

PORTFOLIO ACTIVITY SUMMARY				
Criteria	Portfolio page reference	0–1	1–4	4–7
E.1.a	See pages 19 and 20 for Portfolio Activities			
E.1.b	See page 22 for Portfolio Activity			

E.1 Maintain a child orientated environment

E.1.a, E.1.b – See grid E.1 for cross-referenced knowledge evidence activities.

E.1.1 Maintain the physical environment for young children

	Criteria	Knowledge evidence	Date completed
PROGRESS CHECKLIST	E.1.1.a	Safety requirements with respect to heating, lighting, access, including content of current borough/council regulations and documents.	
	E.1.1.b	Safety procedures for emergencies, including fire.	
	E.1.1.c	Ways in which the layout of furniture and equipment can: 1) encourage or discourage different kinds of activity, including individual work, work and communication in pairs, group activity and cooperation; 2) increase or decrease children's feelings of security; 3) make it physically easier/harder to engage in an activity and clear up mess/change activities.	
	E.1.1.d	Entry to and layout within a setting may create access problems for the physically handicapped.	
	E.1.1.e	The modifications required to the environment to cater for children with a variety of special needs.	
	E.1.1.f	The benefits to young children of being able to participate in decision making.	
	E.1.1.g	Children's need to explore their environment in safety and security.	

USEFUL BOOKS

Accident Prevention in Day Care and Play Settings. Pam Laidman (1992) NES Arnold.

PORTFOLIO ACTIVITY SUMMARY

Criteria	Portfolio page reference	0–1	1–4	4–7
E.1.1.c, d, e	See below for Portfolio Activity			

E.1.1.a   Find out the current borough/council regulations for your workplace. Which department sets these regulations? Where are the relevant documents kept?

....

E.1.1.b   Write down the fire drill in your present placement.

....

E.1.1.c, E.1.1.d, E.1.1.e Portfolio Activity

Design a layout of furniture and equipment for the setting in which you are working. Explain how your design will encourage/discourage different kinds of activity, make it easier/harder to engage in an activity and how it will encourage individual work, paired work and group work/activities. Discuss what modifications you could make to the environment:

   (a) for children with physical disabilities;
   (b) for children with a variety of special needs.

E.1.1.f   What may be the benefits of young children being able to participate in decision making?

....

    How could you encourage their participation?

....

E.1.1.g   Explain why it is important for the carer to reassure young children after changing a play area.

....

    How could you reassure young children before/after a play area has been changed?

....

E.1.2 Maintain an attractive and stimulating environment for young children

<table>
<tr><th rowspan="9" style="writing-mode: vertical-rl">PROGRESS CHECKLIST</th><th>Criteria</th><th>Knowledge evidence</th><th>Date completed</th></tr>
<tr><td>E.1.2.a</td><td>Principles of display: how to arrange materials to attract children's attention, how to make it easier to absorb content.</td><td></td></tr>
<tr><td>E.1.2.b</td><td>A variety of techniques for mounting work and displaying it attractively.</td><td></td></tr>
<tr><td>E.1.2.c</td><td>The names of common plants and materials found in the vicinity.</td><td></td></tr>
<tr><td>E.1.2.d</td><td>How to care for plants.</td><td></td></tr>
</table>

USEFUL BOOKS

Ways to Display – A practical guide for teachers. Derek Greenstreet (1985) Ward Lock.

PORTFOLIO ACTIVITY SUMMARY				
Criteria	Portfolio page reference	0–1	1–4	4–7
E.1.2.c, d	See below for Portfolio Activity			

E.1.2.a   Suggest how you could arrange a display to attract children's attention and help them absorb the content.

....

E.1.2.b   Suggest three ways in which you could mount a child's picture and display it attractively.

....

 ### *E.1.2.c, E.1.2.d Portfolio Activity*

Carry out a nature 'walk' in the vicinity of your workplace. Suggest ways of helping the children to learn the names of common plants and materials found. How could you encourage children to care for plants? Record your ideas.

E.1.3 Maintain a reassuring environment for children

PROGRESS CHECKLIST	Criteria	Knowledge evidence	Date completed
	E.1.3.a	Common sources of fear among babies, toddlers, pre-schoolers, including fear of separation. (This covers simple knowledge of common stage fears – enough to anticipate/recognise, but nothing else.)	
	E.1.3.b	Awareness of manifestations of fear. Ways of reassuring/dealing with fears including use of comfort objects.	
	E.1.3.c	Existence of marked differences among children in liking for/need for physical comfort.	
	E.1.3.d	A variety of equipment and materials, including kitchen and washing equipment, and fabrics (typical of a range of cultural backgrounds).	

USEFUL BOOKS

Special Issues in Child Care. M. O'Hagan and M. Smith (1994) Bailliere Tindall.

PORTFOLIO ACTIVITY SUMMARY

Criteria	Portfolio page reference	0–1	1–4	4–7
E.1.3.c	See page 22 for Portfolio Activity			

E.1.3.a   Although each child has his/her own pattern of behaviour, it can be useful to have a basic knowledge of common stage fears. Suggest which childhood fears are most likely to develop when a child is:

(*a*) 6 months;

....

(*b*) 1 year;

....

(c) 2 years;

....

(d) 3 years;

....

(e) 4 years;

....

(f) 5 years;

....

(g) 6 years;

....

(h) 7 years.

....

(Adapted from *Practical Parenting* **magazine)**

E.1.3.b   Suggest two ways of reassuring/dealing with fear.

....

What role might comfort objects play?

....

E.1.3.c Portfolio Activity

Record two instances you have experienced which show marked differences among children in their liking for/need for physical comfort.

E.1.3.d   How would you make a home corner more appropriate for a child whose second language is English and who has just started at your nursery? What sort of dressing-up clothes would you provide?

....

E.2 MAINTAIN THE SAFETY OF CHILDREN
UNIT WIDE KNOWLEDGE

Criteria	Unit wide knowledge	Date completed
E.2.a	Basic knowledge of children's development 6 weeks to 8 years and importance of taking account of this when considering safety arrangements.	
E.2.b	Awareness of hazards within the environment e.g. traffic, pollution, strangers, animals, poison berries, water etc.	
E.2.c	The need to actively protect children from hazards and the vital role adults have in this.	
E.2.d	The importance of keeping records essential to the safety of children and of ongoing consultation with the primary carer.	
E.2.e	Health and safety requirements of the setting and the importance of ensuring that these are displayed and communicated clearly to other adults in the setting.	
E.2.f	The responsibility of the carer with regard to protection from infectious diseases and the positive contribution immunisation can make.	
E.2.g	Identify and use available resources concerned with safety to raise awareness of candidate, children and adults.	
E.2.h	Provide children, parents and other adults with a positive role model with regard to safety.	

PROGRESS CHECKLIST

USEFUL BOOKS

Babies and Young Children Book 2 – Work and Care. Beaver *et al.* (1995) Stanley Thornes.
Special Issues in Child Care. M. O'Hagan and M. Smith (1994) Balliere Tindall.

 # *Grid E.2*

Please tick box when activity is complete.
P = *Portfolio Activity*

E.2.b	E.2.6.a	E.2.6.b	E.2.6.c	E.2.6.d	E.2.6.e	E.2.6.f
	P	P	P	P	P	P

E.2.c	E.2.5.a	E.2.5.b	E.2.5.c	E.2.5.d	E.2.5.e	E.2.2.a

E.2.e	E.2.1.a	E.2.1.b	E.2.1.c	E.2.1.d	E.2.1.e	E.2.1.f	E.2.2.a
	P					P	

E.2.f	E.2.4.g	E.2.4.h

E.2.g	E.2.3.b	E.2.4.c	E.2.4.d	E.2.4.e	E.2.2.c	E.2.3.a	E.2.4.f
		P				P	

E.2.h	E.2.2.b	E.2.4.a	E.2.4.b

PORTFOLIO ACTIVITY SUMMARY				
Criteria	**Portfolio page reference**	**0–1**	**1–4**	**4–7**
E.2.a	See below for Portfolio Activity			
E.2.b	See page 36 for Portfolio Activity			
E.2.e	See page 27 for Portfolio Activity			
E.2.g	See pages 30 and 32 for Portfolio Activities			

E.2 Maintain the safety of children

E.2.a Portfolio Activity

Present a range of observations which demonstrate your knowledge of children's development from 6 weeks to 8 years and show the importance of taking account of this when considering safety arrangements.

If you have completed C.2.a, there is no need to complete E.2.a but please provide a completion date for C.2.a.

E.2.b, E.2.c, E.2.d, E.2.e, E.2.f, E.2.g, E.2.h – See grid E.2 for cross-referenced knowledge evidence activities.

E.2.1 Maintain a safe environment for children

<table>
<tr><td rowspan="7">PROGRESS CHECKLIST</td><td>Criteria</td><td>Knowledge evidence</td><td>Date completed</td></tr>
<tr><td>E.2.1.a</td><td>The importance of maintaining a hygienic environment for the safety of children.</td><td></td></tr>
<tr><td>E.2.1.b</td><td>Routine safety checks on premises/equipment are carried out and appropriate action as a result of these is taken.</td><td></td></tr>
<tr><td>E.2.1.c</td><td>How to identify potential hazards and minimise possible effects of them within the setting both indoors and outdoors.</td><td></td></tr>
<tr><td>E.2.1.d</td><td>The health and safety hazard posed by animals in the care/education setting.</td><td></td></tr>
<tr><td>E.2.1.e</td><td>The procedures for reporting and correcting any safety hazards as quickly as possible in a manner which does not undermine the confidence of children.</td><td></td></tr>
<tr><td>E.2.1.f</td><td>The importance of adhering to manufacturers' recommendations and relevant safety standards when using equipment.</td><td></td></tr>
</table>

USEFUL BOOKS

Child Care and Development 3rd edition. Pamela Minett (1985) John Murray.

PORTFOLIO ACTIVITY SUMMARY

Criteria	Portfolio page reference	0–1	1–4	4–7
E.2.1.a	See page 27 for Portfolio Activity			
E.2.1.f	See page 27 for Portfolio Activity			

E.2.1.a Portfolio Activity

Design a poster which shows the importance of maintaining a hygienic environment for the safety of children.

E.2.1.b   Give two examples of procedures in the workplace which are set up to ensure safety and state why they are important.

....

What would you do if you discovered a safety hazard?

....

E.2.1.c   Identify three potential hazards in your workplace.

....

Suggest briefly how you could minimise the possible effects of them.

....

E.2.1.d   What precautions would you take with pets in the work setting?

....

E.2.1.e   Describe the procedure of your workplace for reporting and correcting any safety hazards.

....

E.2.1.f Portfolio Activity

Collect as many examples of relevant safety symbols as you can. Which are the most common?

E.2.2 Maintain supervision of children

<table>
<tr><td rowspan="4" style="background:black;color:white;font-weight:bold;">PROGRESS CHECKLIST</td><td>Criteria</td><td>Knowledge evidence</td><td>Date completed</td></tr>
<tr><td>E.2.2.a</td><td>The regulations concerning adult/child ratios appropriate in the setting and the importance of adhering to these.</td><td></td></tr>
<tr><td>E.2.2.b</td><td>That adult anxiety/inappropriate reactions to events are often transmitted to children and that stereotyping can prevent a child from achieving his/her potential.</td><td></td></tr>
<tr><td>E.2.2.c</td><td>The importance of policies and procedures for collection of children taking account of any special circumstances e.g. Care Orders.</td><td></td></tr>
</table>

USEFUL BOOKS

Babies and Young Children Book 2 – Work and Care. Beaver *et al.* (1994) Stanley Thornes.
Special Issues in Child Care. M. O'Hagan and M. Smith. (1994) Bailliere Tindall.

E.2.2.a   What are the regulations concerning adult/child ratios in:

(*a*) day nurseries?

....

(*b*) schools?

....

(*c*) private homes?

....

Why is it important not to exceed these guidelines?

....

E.2.2b   On a warm summer day, the children are sitting in the room, 'cutting and sticking' when suddenly a large wasp flies into the room and lands on your neck and stings you. The child nearest you screams loudly, waving her scissors in the air.

What action would you take? List three from these alternatives in priority order.

(*a*) Leave the room immediately for first aid.
(*b*) Shout for help.
(*c*) Remain calm.
(*d*) Send all the children out to play.
(*e*) Remove scissors from the child.
(*f*) Kill the wasp.
(*g*) Dial 999.
(*h*) Quietly send one of the children to fetch another adult.

....

E.2.2.c   Child 'A' lives with his mother who has a Court Order forbidding the child's father to have any contact with his family. Father arrives and insists he has permission to take his child home.

What would you do? Write down the correct answer.

(*a*) Allow the child to go with his father 'just this once'.
(*b*) Take the child home yourself.
(*c*) Ask father to stay with the child while you go and check with your supervisor.
(*d*) Ask the father to wait while you take the child to check with your supervisor.
(*e*) Ask the father to wait while you take the child to contact the mother.

....

E.2.3 Carry out emergency procedures

PROGRESS CHECKLIST	Criteria	Knowledge evidence	Date completed
	E.2.3.a	The importance of maintaining and using accurate records to enable parents to be contacted quickly if necessary.	
	E.2.3.b	Routine fire/emergency drill and how to respond promptly and appropriately in such situations.	

USEFUL BOOKS

Caring for Young Children. Jennie and Lance Linden (1994) Macmillan.

PORTFOLIO ACTIVITY SUMMARY				
Criteria	Portfolio page reference	0–1	1–4	4–7
E.2.3.a	See below for Portfolio Activity			

 ### E.2.3.a Portfolio Activity

People working in child care must keep accurate records of the children in their care. The essentials are stipulated in The Children's Act. These are:

- *child's name, address and telephone number;*
- *age and date of birth;*
- *name by which child is known and birth name (if different);*
- *surname and name of parents;*
- *emergency telephone numbers;*
- *information about any health problems or conditions and any medication the child takes.*

Local authorities have powers to require additional information to be kept on record.

Design a form to be completed by the nursery when a new child starts attending.

E.2.3.b   Outline the emergency drill at your place of work and state your role in the event of a fire. (If you have already completed this in another unit put unit number and date.)

....

E.2.4 Cope with accidents or injuries to children

	Criteria	Knowledge evidence	Date completed
PROGRESS CHECKLIST	E.2.4.a	Convey information to parents without causing undue alarm.	
	E.2.4.b	How to recognise and cope with the children's emotional reaction to accidents and emergencies.	
	E.2.4.c	Suitable contents of first-aid box for a child care/education setting and the importance of checking contents on a regular basis.	
	E.2.4.d	How to assess the situation quickly and decide if medical attention is required.	
	E.2.4.e	Basic first aid required in an emergency and how to apply it.	
	E.2.4.f	The setting's requirements for recording accidents and emergencies.	
	E.2.4.g	The policies and procedures of the setting for handling and disposing of body fluids and waste material particularly in light of AIDS/HIV virus, hepatitis etc.	
	E.2.4.h	The importance of carrying out standard procedures in the event of an accident in a calm and reassuring manner.	

USEFUL BOOKS

First Aid for Children. Sir Cameron Moffat (1994) Dorling Kindersley.

The British Red Cross and St. John's Ambulance Service may also provide information relating to first aid and children.

PORTFOLIO ACTIVITY SUMMARY

Criteria	Portfolio page reference	0–1	1–4	4–7
E.2.4.c	See below for Portfolio Activity			

E.2.4.a   Scenario: Anil, age three-and-a-half, slips on ice in the playground at lunchtime. He sustains a suspected broken finger and needs to be taken to hospital.

What would you say to the parents on the telephone? Write down the answer you think most appropriate.

(*a*) I don't want to alarm you but we are very worried about Anil, he has had a bad accident.
(*b*) Come quickly, something terrible has happened to Anil!
(*c*) Hello, how are you? We haven't seen you at nursery recently but we need to see you now!
(*d*) Would you come and collect Anil, he's had a fall in the playground.
(*e*) Anil has hurt himself, but don't worry he'll be all right. Could you come as soon as possible?

....

E.2.4.b   Suggest ways of recognising and coping with children's emotional reactions to accidents and emergencies.

....

 ### E.2.4.c Portfolio Activity

Plan what you would include in a first-aid box.

E.2.4.d,   Two children collide outside, both are hurt, one of them seems to be
E.2.4.e,   unconscious. What would you do if you were the first adult on the scene of the
E.2.4.h   accident?

....

You are looking after two children aged three and five in their own home. They are playing happily at dressing-up when you arrive. A few minutes after their parents leave, you go to join the children. You notice the three-year-old has a bottle in her hand. There are two tablets in the bottle and she is happily crunching at something in her mouth. What do you do?

....

E.2.4.f   Record your setting's requirements for recording accidents and emergencies.

....

E.2.4.g   What procedure would you adopt if a child cut its leg which was bleeding badly?

....

E.2.5 Help keep children safe from abuse

<table>
<tr><th></th><th>Criteria</th><th>Knowledge evidence</th><th>Date completed</th></tr>
<tr><td rowspan="6" style="writing-mode: vertical-lr">PROGRESS CHECKLIST</td><td>E.2.5.a</td><td>The physical and emotional signs of physical abuse and neglect and sexual abuse in children.</td><td></td></tr>
<tr><td>E.2.5.b</td><td>The importance of adhering to regulations laid down in the setting with regard to suspected child abuse.</td><td></td></tr>
<tr><td>E.2.5.c</td><td>The boundaries of the candidate's role appropriate to the setting with regard to child abuse and understanding the importance of informing line manager of explanations of injuries given by parent/carer.</td><td></td></tr>
<tr><td>E.2.5.d</td><td>The significance of negative changes in children's behaviour and the importance of observing, recording and reporting this.</td><td></td></tr>
<tr><td>E.2.5.e</td><td>The importance of involving parents/carers from the early stages of enquiries.</td><td></td></tr>
<tr><td>E.2.5.f</td><td>How to observe children while carrying out routines for signs of injuries and abrasions and how and when these are reported.</td><td></td></tr>
</table>

USEFUL BOOKS

Babies and Young Children Book 1 – Development 0–7. Beaver *et al.* (1994) Stanley Thornes.
Babies and Young Children Book 2 – Work and Care. Beaver *et al.* (1995) Stanley Thornes.
Child Protection in Early Childhood Services. (Papers from a conference at the National Children's Bureau.) Ed. G. Pugh and A. Hollows (1994) National Children's Bureau.

E.2.5.a   Give three examples of physical abuse.

....

Give three signs of sexual abuse.

....

Give three signs of a child being neglected.

....

E.2.5.b   What are the regulations in your workplace with regard to child protection?

....

E.2.5.c   What is your role in the workplace with regard to child abuse?

....

Give two reasons why it is important to inform your supervisor of explanations of injuries given by parents.

....

E.2.5.d,   A child's behaviour may change for many reasons. Why then is it important to
E.2.5.e   observe, record and monitor these changes?

....

Are parents/carers always involved in the early stages of enquiries into abuse?

....

Who would be responsible for discussing any concerns regarding suspect abuse with parents?

....

E.2.5.f   What opportunities do you have in the daily routine to observe and identify possible signs and symptoms of abuse?

....

How and to whom should you report?

....

E.2.6 Ensure children's safety on outings

PROGRESS CHECKLIST	Criteria	Knowledge evidence	Date completed
	E.2.6.a	A range of outings suitable for individual age ranges.	
	E.2.6.b	The necessity of obtaining the permission of line manager before taking children off the premises and when it is appropriate to obtain parental permission.	
	E.2.6.c	How to plan and prepare for an outing, with regard to safety, transport requirements, appropriate clothing, food and equipment.	
	E.2.6.d	The regulations including insurance cover regarding the safe transportation of children in private cars.	
	E.2.6.e	The importance of keeping a list of children on an outing and the necessity of checks at regular intervals.	
	E.2.6.f	The contribution parents can make to outings and the importance of giving them full information in advance of the event.	

USEFUL BOOKS

Accident Prevention in Day Care and Play Settings. Pam Laidman (1992) NES Arnold.

PORTFOLIO ACTIVITY SUMMARY

Criteria	Portfolio page reference	0–1	1–4	4–7
E.2.6.a–f	See below for Portfolio Activity			

 E.2.6.a, E.2.6.b, E.2.6.c, E.2.6.d, E.2.6.e, E.2.6.f Portfolio Activity

Choose two outings you consider suitable for the following age groups:

0–1 years;
1–4 years;
4–7 years.

Select one of the above and describe how you would plan and implement the outing. Include who you need to obtain permission from, safety factors, including insurance, ways of checking the children are all present and how you would involve the parents.

P.2 Establish and maintain relationships with the parents of young children

Unit wide knowledge

	Criteria	Unit wide knowledge	Date completed
PROGRESS CHECKLIST	P.2.a	The significance of the central role played by parents in their children's welfare and development.	
	P.2.b	The significance of the bond between parents and their children.	
	P.2.c	The social, environmental and cultural context in which families live.	
	P.2.d	Variations in family values and practices across cultural and other groupings and awareness that practices also vary within such groups.	
	P.2.e	How to communicate with parents as equals, how to listen to parents and how to adjust and modify communication with parents according to their interest, knowledge and confidence.	
	P.2.f	How pressure of parents' circumstances can affect their communication and relationships with their children and with other adults.	
	P.2.g	The importance of establishing positive relationships with parents including the possible barriers to communication and ways of overcoming these.	
	P.2.h	The principles of open communication and the limits and boundaries of confidentiality.	
	P.2.i	The candidate's role and responsibilities with regard to establishing and maintaining relationships with parents and circumstances in which parents should be referred to senior colleagues or other professionals.	

USEFUL BOOKS

Special Issues in Child Care. M. O'Hagan and M. Smith (1994) Bailliere Tindall.

 # *Grid P.2*

Please tick box when activity is complete.
P = *Portfolio Activity*

P.2.a	P.2.1.a	P.2.4.a	P.2.4.b
	P		

P.2.b	P.2.2.a	P.2.2.b	P.2.2.c	P.2.2.d
	P	P	P	P

P.2.c	P.2.2.e
	P

P.2.d	P.2.1.c	P.2.4.c
	P	

P.2.e	P.2.1.b	P.2.3.a	P.2.3.b	P.2.3.c	P.2.3.d
	P		P	P	P

P.2.g	P.2.3.e

P.2.h	P.2.3.f
	P

P.2.i	P.2.1.d	P.2.1.e	P.2.4.d
	P	P	P

PORTFOLIO ACTIVITY SUMMARY

Criteria	Portfolio page reference	0–1	1–4	4–7
P.2.a	See page 42 for Portfolio Activity			
P.2.b	See page 44 for Portfolio Activity			
P.2.c	See page 44 for Portfolio Activity			
P.2.d	See page 42 for Portfolio Activity			
P.2.e	See pages 42 and 46 for Portfolio Activities			
P.2.f	See below for Portfolio Activity			
P.2.h	See page 46 for Portfolio Activity			
P.2.i	See pages 42 and 48 for Portfolio Activities			

P.2 Establish and maintain relationships with parents of young children

P.2.a, P.2.b, P.2.c, P.2.d, P.2.e – See grid P.2 for cross-referenced knowledge evidence activities.

P.2.f Portfolio Activity

It is important for child care workers to realise how pressure of parents' circumstances can affect their communication and relationships with their children and with other adults. Describe two sorts of pressure that parents may face and suggest an action plan for each that may help you to assist them in overcoming these pressures.

P.2.g, P.2.h, P.2.i – See grid P.2 for cross-referenced knowledge evidence activities.

P.2.1 Develop relationships with parents of young children

	Criteria	Knowledge evidence	Date completed
PROGRESS CHECKLIST	P.2.1.a	The concept and implications of shared care and partnership with parents.	
	P.2.1.b	The kinds of information likely to be needed by parents.	
	P.2.1.c	Methods of establishing relationships with parents who are not of the predominant cultural and linguistic group that the carer deals with, including sources of additional help and information.	
	P.2.1.d	The policy of the setting concerning confidentiality of information including rules relating to children under Social Services/Work Supervision and medical records.	
	P.2.1.e	Parents' rights under the relevant legislation.	

USEFUL BOOKS

Your child and the National Curriculum. DFE, HMSO.
How is your child doing at school: a parent's guide to tests and reports for 7-year-olds.
'Involving Ethnic Minority Parents'. (May 1991) *Child Education.*

PORTFOLIO ACTIVITY SUMMARY				
Criteria	Portfolio page reference	0–1	1–4	4–7
P.2.1.a	See page 42 for Portfolio Activity			
P.2.1.b	See page 42 for Portfolio Activity			
P.2.1.c	See page 42 for Portfolio Activity			
P.2.1.d	See page 42 for Portfolio Activity			
P.2.1.e	See page 42 for Portfolio Activity			

P.2.1.a Portfolio Activity

Devise a plan to use in your work setting that encourages partnership with parents, which will help you understand the concept and implications of shared care.

P.2.1.b Portfolio Activity

Design a leaflet giving the information you think a parent may require when they have decided to, or have to send their child to, your work setting.

P.2.1.c Portfolio Activity

Suggest five ways in which your work setting could establish relationships with parents who are not of the predominant cultural or linguistic group, including where you would get additional help from.

P.2.1.d Portfolio Activity

Record the policy of your work setting concerning confidentiality of information. Find out what the rules relating to children are under the social services/work supervision and medical records.

P.2.1.e Portfolio Activity

Find out what legislation is relevant to parents. What are their rights under this legislation?

P.2.2 Implement settling-in arrangements with parots

	Criteria	Knowledge evidence	Date completed
P R O G R E S S C H E C K L I S T	P.2.2.a	How children at different ages are likely to react to separation from parents and transition from one type of setting to another.	
	P.2.2.b	The arrangements for settling in and how to communicate these to parents.	
	P.2.2.c	Differing theories about settling in and separating from parents and their implications for practice.	
	P.2.2.d	Key areas on which clear policies and mutual agreement should be established e.g. routines, boundary setting, emergencies.	
	P.2.2.e	The difficulties faced by children and parents whose cultural and language background is different from the predominant culture and language of the setting.	

USEFUL BOOKS

Special Issues in Child Care. M. O'Hagan and M. Smith (1993) Bailliere Tindall.
'Making the Break'. H. Moritimer (1983) *Child Education.*
'Preparing Children for School'. R. Rees and M. E. Young (September 1981) *Health Visitor* (Vol. 54).

PORTFOLIO ACTIVITY SUMMARY

Criteria	Portfolio page reference	0–1	1–4	4–7
P.2.2.a–e	See page 44 for Portfolio Activity			

P.2.2.a, P.2.2.b, P.2.2.c, P.2.2.d, P.2.2.e Portfolio Activity

You have been given a list of names of children who are about to begin at your work setting.

- *(a) Devise a number of questions which you feel may be useful in assessing the level of children's (un)preparedness for the first few days.*
- *(b) Write an itinerary for an introductory visit by parents and children.*
- *(c) Describe two different theories about settling in and separating from parents and their implications for practice.*
- *(d) Suggest key areas on which clear policies and mutual agreement should be established and give your ideas on how this may be achieved.*
- *(e) Devise strategies for dealing with the difficulties faced by the children and the parents whose cultural and language background is different from the predominant culture and language of your setting.*

P.2.3 Exchange information with parents about their children

	Criteria	Knowledge evidence	Date completed
PROGRESS CHECKLIST	P.2.3.a	Why exchange of information is beneficial to parent, children and staff.	
	P.2.3.b	The types of information needed from parents and how to obtain it, record it and keep it up to date.	
	P.2.3.c	The types of information needed by parents and how to communicate it effectively.	
	P.2.3.d	Strategies for sharing and exchange of information which takes account of the need for flexibility and sensitive negotiation with parents.	
	P.2.3.e	Barriers to effective communication.	
	P.2.3.f	How to keep records of information, confidential nature of some information and who has access to records.	

USEFUL BOOKS

Working with Parents. John Bastiani (1992) Routledge.

PORTFOLIO ACTIVITY SUMMARY

Criteria	Portfolio page reference	0–1	1–4	4–7
P.2.3.b–d	See page 46 for Portfolio Activity			
P.2.3.f	See page 46 for Portfolio Activity			

P.2.3.a   Why is the exchange of information beneficial to parent, children and staff?

....

P.2.3.b, P.2.3.c, P.2.3.d Portfolio Activity

Make a list of information needed from parents and describe how you will obtain it, record it and keep it up to date. Make a list of information that parents will need and describe your strategies for communicating it effectively. Suggest three strategies for sharing and exchanging information with parents which allow for flexibility and negotiation.

P.2.3.e   List five barriers to effective communication.

....

P.2.3.f Portfolio Activity

Design an information record sheet for a child highlighting which information could be confidential. Describe who will have access to this information and how and where it will be stored.

P.2.4 Share the care and management of children with their parents

	Criteria	Knowledge evidence	Date completed
PROGRESS CHECKLIST	P.2.4.a	The worker's role in the care and management of children and in sharing this with parents.	
	P.2.4.b	The central role of parents in the care and management of their children.	
	P.2.4.c	Rationale for policies pursued by the setting and ways in which family values may differ from those of the setting.	
	P.2.4.d	Health and safety procedures with regard to different types of emergencies including accidents, illness, emergency closure of the setting etc. and when and how to contact parents.	

USEFUL BOOKS

Accident Prevention in Day Care and Play Settings. Pam Laidman (1992) NES Arnold.
Special Issues in Child Care. M. O'Hagan and M. Smith (1993) Bailliere Tindall.

PORTFOLIO ACTIVITY SUMMARY				
Criteria	Portfolio page reference	0–1	1–4	4–7
P.2.4.d	See page 48 for Portfolio Activity			

P.2.4.a   What is the role of the worker in sharing the care and management of children with their parents?

....

P.2.4.b   What is the role of parents in the care and management of their children?

....

P.2.4.c   State three ways in which family values may differ from the policies of the work setting and suggest how you would overcome them.

....

 ### *P.2.4.d Portfolio Activity*

Record the policy of your work setting with regard to different types of emergencies including when and how to contact parents.

C.3 PROMOTE THE PHYSICAL DEVELOPMENT OF YOUNG CHILDREN
UNIT WIDE KNOWLEDGE

—

Criteria	Unit wide knowledge	Date completed
C.3.a	A knowledge of children's physical development 6 weeks to 8 years and how this relates to other aspects of their development.	
C.3.b	The necessity for a gradual introduction to physical activity, building on the child's previous experience.	
C.3.c	The different types of play and the potential of play provision in the promotion of the physical development of young children.	
C.3.d	The wide variety of rates of physical development of children.	
C.3.e	Observation, recording and evaluation of the physical development of children.	
C.3.f	The underlying needs which are necessary to enable the child to thrive (e.g. diet, rest, sleep, fresh air).	
C.3.g	The factors necessary to create a healthy indoor and outdoor environment for the child making maximum use of space available.	
C.3.h	How to plan, implement and evaluate activities which promote and extend physical development, confidence, independence and co-operation according to the child's level of development.	
C.3.i	The importance of suitable clothing for physical activity having regard for cultural and religious considerations.	

PROGRESS CHECKLIST

C.3.j	The Health and Safety policies of the setting and their application showing an awareness of the necessity for constant supervision.	
C.3.k	Set up activities for children and use strategies which foster involvement regardless of gender, race or culture and understand the rationale for this.	
C.3.l	Adapt provision to cater for the needs of children who have difficulties/special needs.	
C.3.m	Provide assistance for children while allowing them to maintain control over their activity.	
C.3.n	The importance of the child's need for choice in participation in activities and use of equipment.	

USEFUL BOOKS

Babies and Young Children Book 1 – Development 0–7. Beaver *et al.* (1994) Stanley Thornes.
Caring for the Under 8s. Jennie and Lance Linden (1993) Macmillan.
From Birth to Five Years. M. Sheridan (1987) NFER Nelson.
The Growth and Development of Children. Catherine Lee (1989) Longman.

✓ Grid C.3

Please tick box when activity is complete.
P = *Portfolio Activity*

C.3.a	C.3.1.a	C.3.1.b	C.3.1.c
	P	P	P

C.3.b	C.3.2.a
	P

C.3.c	C.3.3.g

C.3.d	C.3.3.h
	P

C.3.h	C.3.3.b	C.3.3.c	C.3.3.d
	P	P	P

C.3.j	C.3.3.a
	P

C.3.l	C.3.2.b	C.3.3.e	C.3.3.f

C.3.m	C.3.4.a	C.3.4.b
	P	P

C.3.n	C.3.4.c	C.3.4.d
	P	P

PORTFOLIO ACTIVITY SUMMARY

Criteria	Portfolio page reference	0–1	1–4	4–7
C.3.a	See pages 53 and 55 for Portfolio Activities			
C.3.b	See page 56 for Portfolio Activity			
C.3.d	See page 59 for Portfolio Activity			
C.3.e	See page 53 for Portfolio Activity			
C.3.f	See page 53 for Portfolio Activity			
C.3.h	See page 59 for Portfolio Activity			
C.3.i	See page 54 for Portfolio Activity			
C.3.j	See page 59 for Portfolio Activity			
C.3.k	See page 54 for Portfolio Activity			
C.3.m	See page 60 for Portfolio Activity			
C.3.n	See page 61 for Portfolio Activity			

C.3 Promote the physical development of young children

C.3.a Portfolio Activity

'Development involves four aspects: physical, intellectual, emotional and social and each is dependent on the other.' Extract from Patricia Geraghty's Caring for Young Children.

Read Mary Sheridan's and Catherine Lee's books on development.

Design a booklet for a parent explaining in detail the general development of a child aged 0–8 years. Outline the role of the adult in promoting physical development in children. The booklet should have sections on the following ages:

> *0–1 years;*
> *1–4 years;*
> *4–7 years.*

For each age use these subheadings:

- *physical;*
- *intellectual;*
- *emotional;*
- *social.*

C.3.a, C.3.f Portfolio Activity

Children have certain basic physical and psychological needs. Find out about Maslow's 'hierarchy of needs' in Human Development, *(Muller 1992).*

> *(a) What are the basic physical needs in children? Discuss in detail.*
> *(b) How can the carer meet these physical needs? Discuss in detail.*
> *(c) What are the basic psychological needs in children?*
> *(d) How can the carer meet these psychological needs?*
> *(e) Discuss the 'underlying needs' necessary in order that the child may thrive. Prepare detailed notes for reference.*

C.3.b, C.3.c, C.3.d – See grid C.3 for cross-referenced knowledge evidence activities.

C.3.e Portfolio Activity

Choose one child from each of the following age groups: 0–1, 1–4, 4–7 years and observe an indoor or outdoor activity. Assess the developmental capabilities of each child. Record and evaluate.

C.3.g   What factors would you consider necessary to create a healthy environment

(*a*) indoors?

(b) outdoors?

....

How would you maximise the use of space available?

....

C.3.h – See grid C.3 for cross-referenced knowledge evidence activities.

 ### *C.3.i, C.3.k Portfolio Activity*

Set up two physical activities for children, one indoors and one outdoors.

    (a) What was the type and nature of the clothing worn? In detail, discuss appropriateness of clothing.

    (b) Discuss strategies used to get children involved in activities regardless of gender, race or culture.

    (c) How much or how little control did you have during the activity with the children? Give rationale. Make reference to activity and use of equipment.

    (d) Discuss 'constant supervision' of children during activity.

    (e) Explain, in full, the Health and Safety policies of your work setting with children.

C.3.j, C.3.l, C.3.m, C.3.n – See grid C.3 for cross-referenced knowledge evidence activities.

C.3.1 Help children to develop confidence in movement

Criteria	Knowledge evidence	Date completed
C.3.1.a	How to communicate verbally and non-verbally to encourage children's vocabulary about movement and spatial awareness.	
C.3.1.b	How to show approval for children's efforts.	
C.3.1.c	Appropriate activities and equipment and their potential in exploring movement with children.	

USEFUL BOOKS

Special Issues in Child Care. M. O'Hagan and M. Smith (1993) Bailliere Tindall.
Babies and Young Children Book 1 – Development 0–7. Beaver *et al.* (1994) Stanley Thornes.
Caring for the Under 8s. Jennie and Lance Linden (1993) Macmillan.

PORTFOLIO ACTIVITY SUMMARY

Criteria	Portfolio page reference	0–1	1–4	4–7
C.3.1.a, b, c	See below for Portfolio Activity			

C.3.1.a, C.3.1.b, C.3.1.c Portfolio Activity

Plan and implement a movement session with children aged:

> (a) 1 year;
> (b) 3 years;
> (c) 6 years.

Observe them and write a detailed report including an evaluation and modifications, if any. Include:

> (a) Words, questions and actions you would use to encourage children to talk about movement and spatial awareness.
> (b) How you would show children that you are pleased with their efforts.
> (c) Details of the equipment that you would use with children and what they would gain from it.
> (d) The role of the adult in helping children of one, three and six years to develop confidence in movement.

C.3.2 Help children to develop skills of locomotion and balance

<table>
<tr><td rowspan="3" style="writing-mode:vertical">PROGRESS CHECKLIST</td><td>Criteria</td><td>Knowledge evidence</td><td>Date completed</td></tr>
<tr><td>C.3.2.a</td><td>How to extend the children's understanding of the activities they are involved in.</td><td></td></tr>
<tr><td>C.3.2.b</td><td>How to recognise variations from developmental norms and use appropriate referral processes.</td><td></td></tr>
</table>

USEFUL BOOKS

Caring for the Under 8s. Jennie and Lance Linden (1993) Macmillan.
Babies and Young Children Book 1 – Development 0–7. M. Beaver *et al.* (1994) Stanley Thornes.

PORTFOLIO ACTIVITY SUMMARY

Criteria	Portfolio page reference	0–1	1–4	4–7
C.3.2.a	See below for Portfolio Activity			

C.3.2.a Portfolio Activity

Set up some activities to develop skills for locomotion and balance with two- and three-year-olds. Implement and record. Include an evaluation and make some recommendations. Record should provide an answer to the following question:

How did you explain to the group the reasons for doing the activities they were involved in?

C.3.2.b   Find out as much as you can about locomotion and balance problems.

(*a*) What are the problems that a child receiving specialist help may have?

....

(*b*) Who are the specialists in this area and what are the referral procedures?

....

In promoting locomotion and balance, how would the following affect your choice of activities:

(*a*) one-to-one?

....

(*b*) small groups?

....

(*c*) large groups?

....

(*d*) What factors would you take into consideration when designing a programme to help a child with locomotion and balance problems?

....

(*e*) What team games (specify) would you choose to help develop skills in balance and locomotion for the following:

    (*a*) 0–4 years – indoors, no equipment?

    ....

    (*b*) 4–7 years – outdoors, with equipment?

    ....

C.3.3 Help children to development gross manipulative skills

<table>
<tr><td rowspan="9" style="writing-mode: vertical">PROGRESS CHECKLIST</td><td>**Criteria**</td><td>**Knowledge evidence**</td><td>**Date completed**</td></tr>
<tr><td>C.3.3.a</td><td>The uses, safety factors and age appropriateness of a range of apparatus and its potential in helping children to develop gross manipulative skills.</td><td></td></tr>
<tr><td>C.3.3.b</td><td>A range of age appropriate activities and games which may be used in helping children to develop gross manipulative skills.</td><td></td></tr>
<tr><td>C.3.3.c</td><td>The relationship between apparatus/activities/games and the specific physical skills they may help to develop.</td><td></td></tr>
<tr><td>C.3.3.d</td><td>A range of strategies to encourage the participation of all children in activities which will help to develop gross manipulative skills.</td><td></td></tr>
<tr><td>C.3.3.e</td><td>Adaptations to standard equipment for use by children with difficulties/special needs.</td><td></td></tr>
<tr><td>C.3.3.f</td><td>The potential use of wheeled toys, standard and adapted, for use by children with special needs e.g. mobility problems.</td><td></td></tr>
<tr><td>C.3.3.g</td><td>The potential for physical development in such activities as swimming and parachute games.</td><td></td></tr>
<tr><td>C.3.3.h</td><td>Opportunities for the development of gross manipulative skills which occur incidentally and how to use them as they occur.</td><td></td></tr>
</table>

USEFUL BOOKS

Caring for the Under 8s. Jennie and Lance Linden (1993) Macmillan.
Babies and Young Children Book I – Development 0–7. M. Beaver *et al.* (1994) Stanley Thornes.

PORTFOLIO ACTIVITY SUMMARY		0–1	1–4	4–7
Criteria	**Portfolio page reference**			
C.3.3.a	See below for Portfolio Activity			
C.3.3.b, c, d	See below for Portfolio Activity			
C.3.3.h	See below for Portfolio Activity			

C.3.3.a Portfolio Activity

Devise a booklet explaining how types of equipment (see a–d below) help a child to develop gross manipulative skills. Refer to the appropriate age group and size of group. Give reasons for your choice of equipment. Include the safety factors of each piece of equipment and the need for supervision as required by the setting.

> *(a) large equipment;*
> *(b) small equipment;*
> *(c) adapted equipment;*
> *(d) soft and hard objects.*

C.3.3.b, C.3.3.c, C.3.3.d Portfolio Activity

Plan and implement four activities/games to be used with children. Discuss and evaluate. Include:

> *(a) description of specific skills they help to develop in children;*
> *(b) explanation of how you encouraged the children's participation.*

C.3.3.e   How can you adapt equipment which is standard to provide for the needs of children with special needs or difficulties?

....

C.3.3.f   Give a full explanation of how toys with wheels can help the development of children with mobility problems.

....

C.3.3.g   Describe in full how swimming and parachute games encourage physical development in children.

....

C.3.3.h Portfolio Activity

Discuss how the size of group and children's varied rates of development affect your planning of activities to promote gross manipulative skills.

C.3.4 Help children to develop fine manipulative skills

<table>
<tr><td rowspan="5" style="writing-mode: vertical-lr;">PROGRESS CHECKLIST</td><td>**Criteria**</td><td>**Knowledge evidence**</td><td>**Date completed**</td></tr>
<tr><td>C.3.4.a</td><td>How to recognise and take advantage of opportunities for children to practise their manipulative skills as they arise.</td><td></td></tr>
<tr><td>C.3.4.b</td><td>The importance of hand–eye co-ordination and manipulative skills in the development of formal educational skills such as writing.</td><td></td></tr>
<tr><td>C.3.4.c</td><td>A range of tools, implements, materials and activities useful in the development of manipulative skills and the rationale behind their use.</td><td></td></tr>
<tr><td>C.3.4.d</td><td>The contribution that the use of free creative activities make to the development of children's manipulative skills.</td><td></td></tr>
</table>

USEFUL BOOKS

Caring for the Under 8s. Jennie and Lance Linden (1993) Macmillan.

PORTFOLIO ACTIVITY SUMMARY

Criteria	Portfolio page reference	0–1	1–4	4–7
C.3.4.a, b	See below for Portfolio Activity			
C.3.4.c	See page 61 for Portfolio Activity			
C.3.4.d	See page 61 for Portfolio Activity			

 ### C.3.4.a, C.3.4.b Portfolio Activity

Observe children daily in your placement.

>   (a) *What opportunities do you use to help them to develop their fine manipulative skills?*
>   (b) *Describe how hand–eye co-ordination and manipulative skills are related to mark making.*

C.3.4.c Portfolio Activity

Draw up a chart explaining which toys/tasks/activities would help a child with/without special needs to develop fine manipulative skills, ages:

> (a) *0–4 years;*
> (b) *4–7 years.*

What is the role of the adult in:

> (a) *helping the child to develop hand–eye co-ordination?*
> (b) *helping a child who prefers to use his/her left hand when writing and cutting?*

C.3.4.d Portfolio Activity

Set up some activities to help children to develop fine manipulative skills.

> (a) *How can you use free creative activities to encourage children to develop fine manipulative skills?*
> (b) *Describe set tasks in the routine which you would use to help children develop fine manipulative skills. What is the rationale?*

C.5 PROMOTE CHILDREN'S SOCIAL AND EMOTIONAL DEVELOPMENT
UNIT WIDE KNOWLEDGE

	Criteria	Unit wide knowledge	Date completed
PROGRESS CHECKLIST	C.5.a	Basic knowledge of children's social and emotional development 6 weeks to 8 years and how this relates to other aspects of their development.	
	C.5.b	Observation of children and use of information gained to evaluate children's social and emotional development.	
	C.5.c	The basic pattern of social and emotional development in children and recognition of socially acceptable behaviour.	
	C.5.d	The needs of children with respect to social and emotional development and how these needs may be met.	
	C.5.e	How a child's previous early experience affects his/her individual needs and can shape early attitudes and behaviour.	
	C.5.f	Social and environmental factors which could have an adverse effect on children's emotional and social development.	
	C.5.g	How children under stress can regress socially and emotionally.	
	C.5.h	How stereotypical views in carers can hinder the growth of children's independence and their emotional and social development.	

C.5.i	A range of activities and intervention strategies which support and encourage social and emotional development in children.	
C.5.j	The role of play and its potential as an aid to social and emotional development.	
C.5.k	The effects on children's social and emotional development of lack of play opportunities.	
C.5.l	Recognition of racist, sexist, abusive and anti-social behaviour and the effects this has on children's social and emotional development.	
C.5.m	How to challenge racist, sexist, abusive and anti-social behaviour.	
C.5.n	The need to offer comfort and support wherever appropriate.	
C.5.o	How a child's special needs will affect his/her social and emotional development.	
C.5.p	The particular difficulties which may affect the social and emotional development of children who use more than one language.	

USEFUL BOOKS

From Birth to Five Years. M. Sheridan (1987) NFER Nelson.
Keeping the Peace. Susanne Wichert (1989) NSP.
Babies and Young Children Book 1 – Development 0–7. M. Beaver *et al.* (1994) Stanley Thornes.

✓ *Grid C.5*

Please tick box when activity is complete.
P = *Portfolio Activity*

C.5.a	C.5.6.a
	P

C.5.b	C.5.2.c	C.5.4.e
	P	

C.5.c	C.5.3.j	C.5.3.b	C.5.3.c	C.5.3.d	C.5.3.e	C.5.2.e
	P		P	P		

C.5.d	C.5.1.a	C.5.4.a	C.5.4.d	C.5.5.d
	P	P		P

C.5.e	C.5.4.h	C.5.4.b	C.5.2.d
	P	P	

C.5.f	C.5.3.a	C.5.5.h	C.5.4.h	C.5.4.d	C.5.5.b	C.5.5.c
		P				

C.5.g	C.5.4.c	C.5.3.g

C.5.h	C.5.5.i	C.5.6.l	C.5.1.c	C.5.3.k	C.5.6.h	C.5.2.b	C.5.4.f

C.5.i	C.5.3.h	C.5.2.a	C.5.2.h	C.5.3.e	C.5.5.f	C.5.6.f	C.5.2.g	C.5.2.f	C.5.6.e
		P	P		P		P		

C.5.j	C.5.6.i	C.5.4.g
		P

C.5.l	C.5.3.f	C.5.6.b

C.5.m	C.5.6.g	C.5.6.j	C.5.1.b
	P		P

C.5.n	C.5.3.i	C.5.5.a	C.5.5.g	C.5.5.e	C.5.2.i
				P	P	

C.5.o	C.5.6.k	C.5.6.c
		P

C.5.p	C.5.6.d
	P

PORTFOLIO ACTIVITY SUMMARY

Criteria	Portfolio page reference	0–1	1–4	4–7
C.5.a	See page 80 for Portfolio Activity			
C.5.b	See page 70 for Portfolio Activity			
C.5.c	See pages 73 and 74 for Portfolio Activities			
C.5.d	See pages 67, 76 and 78 for Portfolio Activities			
C.5.e	See page 76 for Portfolio Activity			
C.5.f	See page 78 for Portfolio Activity			
C.5.i	See pages 70, 78 and 81 for Portfolio Activities			
C.5.j	See page 76 for Portfolio Activity			
C.5.k	See page 66 for Portfolio Activity			
C.5.m	See pages 67 and 81 for Portfolio Activities			
C.5.n	See page 78 for Portfolio Activity			
C.5.o	See page 81 for Portfolio Activity			
C.5.p	See page 81 for Portfolio Activity			

C.5 Promote children's social and emotional development

C.5.a, C.5.b, C.5.c, C.5.d, C.5.e, C.5.f, C.5.g, C.5.h, C.5.i, C.5.j – See grid C.5 for cross-referenced knowledge evidence activities.

 ### C.5.k Portfolio Activity

What may be the effects of lack of play opportunities on children's social and emotional development? Suggest strategies that you could use to overcome this.

C.5.l, C.5.m, C.5.n, C.5.o, C.5.p – See grid C.5 for cross-referenced knowledge evidence activities.

C.5.1 Help children to relate to others

PROGRESS CHECKLIST	Criteria	Knowledge evidence	Date completed
	C.5.1.a	The individual needs with regard to social and emotional development of the children in the setting, and ways of meeting these needs.	
	C.5.1.b	The role of the adult in the resolution of conflict situations among children and the rationale behind it.	
	C.5.1.c	The importance of adults as role models.	

USEFUL BOOKS

From Birth to Five Years. M. Sheridan (1987) NFER Nelson.
Keeping the Peace. Susanne Wichert (1989) NSP.
Babies and Young Children Book 1 – Development 0–7. M. Beaver *et al.* (1994) Stanley Thornes.

PORTFOLIO ACTIVITY SUMMARY				
Criteria	Portfolio page reference	0–1	1–4	4–7
C.5.1.a	See below for Portfolio Activity			
C.5.1.b	See below for Portfolio Activity			

C.5.1.a Portfolio Activity

Think about the social and emotional needs of two of the children in the setting in which you are working. Plan an activity which will help you meet their needs. Implement the activity and evaluate how successful your ideas were.

C.5.1.b Portfolio Activity

The adult plays an important role in the resolution of conflict situations among children. Describe two conflict situations, one where you have intervened and one when you have not. Give reasons why you did/did not intervene. Evaluate the outcomes.

C.5.1.c,   Complete the spidergram in ten minutes.
C.5.2.b

Why do you feel it is necessary for people who work with children to have good self-esteem?

....

Why is it important for children to have adults as role models?

....

C.5.2 Help children to develop self-reliance and self-esteem

PROGRESS CHECKLIST	Criteria	Knowledge evidence	Date completed
	C.5.2.a	A range of activities, routines and strategies which encourage respect for the individual child and understanding the rationale behind these.	
	C.5.2.b	The importance of self-respect among adult workers and of knowledge of self.	
	C.5.2.c	The development of self-reliance and self-esteem as a gradual process and how this is affected by maturation and the development of communication skills in the child.	
	C.5.2.d	The importance of communication with and knowing how to listen to and encourage interaction between children, and adults and children.	
	C.5.2.e	When it is appropriate to give responsibility to children, why this is important, and that family/cultural expectations of this may vary and should be handled sensitively.	
	C.5.2.f	When to praise a child for his/her efforts and the rationale behind positive reinforcement for effort.	
	C.5.2.g	A range of strategies to encourage negotiation with children, know their possible outcomes and understand the need for flexibility in their application.	
	C.5.2.h	How to provide activities and strategies to promote self-reliance and self-esteem and how they may be adjusted to take account of children from different cultural backgrounds, genders and with special needs.	
	C.5.2.i	How to interact with parents in a manner which reinforces the self-image of the child and the adult and supports positive interaction between parents and child.	

USEFUL BOOKS

From Birth to Five Years. M. Sheridan (1987) NFER Nelson.
Babies and Young Children Book 1 – Development 0–7. M. Beaver *et al.* (1994) Stanley Thornes.
Childcare Research: Policy and Practice. B. Kahan (1989) Hodder and Stoughton.
Childcare: Concerns and Conflicts. S. Morgan and P. Righton (1989) Hodder and Stoughton.

PORTFOLIO ACTIVITY SUMMARY		0–1	1–4	4–7
Criteria	**Portfolio page reference**			
C.5.2.a, h	See below for Portfolio Activity			
C.5.2.c	See below for Portfolio Activity			
C.5.2.g	See page 71 for Portfolio Activity			

C.5.2.a, C.5.2.h, C.5.6.f Portfolio Activity

Design and use a work plan which explores issues of self-image and identity in accordance with appropriate developmental levels. Discuss why it may be difficult for some children to develop a positive self-image and identity.

C.5.2.b   See C.5.1.c on page 68.

C.5.2.c Portfolio Activity

Observe three children – one each in the following age ranges: 0–1, 1–4 and 4–7 years. Compare their development of self-reliance and self-esteem. How is it affected by maturation and the development of communication skills?

C.5.2.d   Think of an activity you could use to encourage interaction between children and adults and children. Give an example of an appropriate piece of equipment you could use and suggest the most beneficial way of using it.

....

C.5.2.e   Suggest when it is appropriate to give children responsibility.

....

How may family/cultural expectations vary?

....

Suggest ideas for a responsibility chart.

....

C.5.2.f   Describe an incident in your workplace/setting where you have praised a child for effort. How did you do this and why?

....

C.5.2.g *Portfolio Activity*

Devise two strategies you could use to encourage negotiation with children.

Implement them and record your findings.

C.5.2.i   Suggest a piece of information which you may have to give to a parent about their child's achievements during the day.

....

Describe the manner in which you could give that information to the parent which reinforces the self-image of the child and would support positive interaction between parent and child.

....

C.5.3 Help children recognise and deal with their feelings

	Criteria	Knowledge evidence	Date completed
PROGRESS CHECKLIST	C.5.3.a	Social and emotional factors which affect children and families.	
	C.5.3.b	The wide range of emotions, both positive and negative, covered by the term 'feeling'.	
	C.5.3.c	The importance for the child's social and emotional development of learning to recognise, name and deal with their feelings and the feelings of others.	
	C.5.3.d	The powerful nature of feelings in young children and what expectations of control would be appropriate.	
	C.5.3.e	Strategies for encouraging the expression of positive and negative feelings in words and actions where appropriate.	
	C.5.3.f	Expression of feeling should not be governed by cultural or gender stereotypes.	
	C.5.3.g	Recognition of signs of distress in a child.	
	C.5.3.h	Recognition of emotional outbursts and negative reactions and appropriate strategies which lead to positive outcomes.	
	C.5.3.i	The rationale behind a calm and reassuring manner when dealing with children who are emotionally upset, including awareness of safety and minimum disruption to other children.	
	C.5.3.j	Learning opportunities which arise in the daily routine to help children who are emotionally upset, including awareness of safety and minimum disruption to other children.	
	C.5.3.k	The role of the carer and boundaries of confidentiality with regard to the sharing of concern about children's emotional and social development with parents, colleagues and other professionals.	

USEFUL BOOKS

Childcare: Concerns and Conflicts. S. Morgan and P. Righton (1989) Hodder and Stoughton.
'Mummy I'm frightened'. *Practical Parenting* (March 1993).
Teacher Timesavers. Pat Gooch (1993) Scholastic.
Childcare Research: Policy and Practice. B. Kahan (1989) Hodder and Stoughton.

PORTFOLIO ACTIVITY SUMMARY				
Criteria	Portfolio page reference	0–1	1–4	4–7
C.5.3.c, d	See below for Portfolio Activity			
C.5.3.j	See page 74 for Portfolio Activity			

C.5.3.a   Gather information on social and environmental factors affecting both children and families. Which appear to be the most common?

....

C.5.3.b   Feelings cover a wide range of emotions, both positive and negative. Describe the wide range of emotions that you have felt over the last week.

....

C.5.3.c, C.5.3.d Portfolio Activity

Plan an activity that would encourage a small group of young children to recognise, name and deal with their feelings and the feelings of others. Describe your expectations of the level and control that would be appropriate for their age and stage of development. Implement the activity and compare your expectations with your results.

C.5.3.e   See C.5.3.h on page 74.

C.5.3.f,   Suggest an implementation plan for the work setting to encourage
C.5.6.b,   understanding about the customs and cultural backgrounds of black and
C.5.6.h   ethnic minority children for both adults and children. Pay particular attention to their needs in a predominantly white society. Include ideas for avoiding sex-role stereotyping. What information can you find out about the relevant legislation?

....

C.5.3.g,   Make a list of your observations of how children who are distressed appear in
C.5.4.c   your workplace/setting.

....

How do you recognise symptoms of distress?

....

C.5.3.e,   Encouraging children to express their feelings through words and pictures can
C.5.3.h   be a useful strategy. What other strategies could you use to encourage children
to express positive and negative feelings, which would turn their emotional
outbursts and negative reactions into positive outcomes?

....

C.5.3.i   When dealing with emotionally upset children, how can you ensure safety and
minimum disruption to others? What is the rationale behind a calm and
reassuring manner from the adult?

....

C.5.3.j Portfolio Activity

*Devise a plan which can be built into the workplace routine that can help children express, discuss
and control their feelings. What strategies could you use for maximising the potential of these learning
opportunities to help children develop socially and emotionally?*

C.5.3.k,   Think about an important piece of information which might have to be raised
C.5.4.f,   with a parent and then a decision reached. How could you take into account
C.5.5.i   the importance of parental involvement in the decision-making process?

....

C.5.4 *Prepare children for moving on to new settings*

	Criteria	Knowledge evidence	Date completed
PROGRESS CHECKLIST	C.5.4.a	Children's needs with regard to change and the importance of preparing for and managing transitions.	
	C.5.4.b	Knowledge of child care/education provision available.	
	C.5.4.c	The effects of separation and how this can affect young children.	
	C.5.4.d	The carer's own role and that of the others involved in arrangements and what action is appropriate to minimise stress in transitions.	
	C.5.4.e	The level of understanding of the child and the importance of giving them information according to this level.	
	C.5.4.f	The importance of parental involvement in decision making.	
	C.5.4.g	Appropriate play activities to encourage positive expectations of the new setting and the role of the carer in these activities.	
	C.5.4.h	The importance of recognising and making use of opportunities to familiarise children with new settings.	

USEFUL BOOKS

'Ready, Steady, off to School'. *Practical Parenting* (September 1992).
'First Time Fears'. *Mother and Baby* (January 1992).
Bright ideas for early years – getting started. L. Mort and J. Morris (1989) Scholastic.
From Birth to Five Years. M. Sheridan (1987) NFER Nelson.
Childcare: Concerns and Conflicts. S. Morgan and P. Righton (1989) Hodder and Stoughton.

PORTFOLIO ACTIVITY SUMMARY		0–1	1–4	4–7
Criteria	**Portfolio page reference**			
C.5.4.a	See below for Portfolio Activity			
C.5.4.b, g, h	See below for Portfolio Activity			

C.5.4.a Portfolio Activity

Think about the needs of the children in your workplace/setting with regard to change and the importance of preparing for and managing transitions. Suggest a plan which would meet their needs.

C.5.4.b, C.5.4.g, C.5.4.h, C.5.5.d, C.5.5.e, C.5.5.f, C.5.5.g, C.5.5.h Portfolio Activity

Devise a familiarisation programme. State the ages of the children, the care/education available and the methods of welcoming. Suggest strategies for recognising individual needs of both adults and children.

Discuss how you will prepare children and adults in the new setting to receive newcomers. Give reasons for the need for flexibility. Include appropriate play activities to encourage positive expectations that are appropriate for the child's level of development and take account of their emotional state.

C.5.4.c   See C.5.3.g on page 74.

C.5.4.d   Think about the role of the care worker in making arrangements to accept new children. What action could be appropriate in helping to minimise stress in transitions?

....

C.5.4.e   Suggest a book which would give information to a child who is afraid of the dark, making sure that the information is appropriate to his/her level of understanding. Write a review of the book.

....

C.5.4.f   See C.5.3.k on page 74.

C.5.5 Help children adjust to the care/education setting

	Criteria	Knowledge evidence	Date completed
PROGRESS CHECKLIST	C.5.5.a	Awareness of young children's needs in relation to change and separation and that these may vary with individuals.	
	C.5.5.b	The effects of change and the importance of sympathetic and appropriate handling including physical contact.	
	C.5.5.c	Sensitivity to the role played by transitional objects and activities as agreed with parents.	
	C.5.5.d	The importance of, and method of, welcoming children and recognising their individual needs.	
	C.5.5.e	The importance of a familiarisation programme which takes into consideration both the level of development of the child and his/her emotional state.	
	C.5.5.f	The rationale behind the strategies of the care/education setting for settling in children and the need for flexibility.	
	C.5.5.g	How children differ in the time taken to adjust to the care/education setting and the different types and levels of support required.	
	C.5.5.h	The importance of preparing children and adults in the new setting to receive newcomers.	
	C.5.5.i	How to impart information to parents in a manner which does not raise anxiety but nevertheless alerts them to potential or actual causes for concern.	

USEFUL BOOKS

Childcare: Concerns and Conflicts. S. Morgan and P. Righton (1989) Hodder and Stoughton.
Bright ideas for early years – getting started. L. Mort and J. Morris (1989) Scholastic.
From Birth to Five Years. M. Sheridan (1987) NFER Nelson.

PORTFOLIO ACTIVITY SUMMARY

Criteria	Portfolio page reference	0–1	1–4	4–7
C.5.5.d, e, f, g, h	See below for Portfolio Activity			

C.5.5.a, C.5.5.b   Why is it important to offer sympathetic appropriate handling, including physical contact, to children undergoing change? When would it not be appropriate? What effects may change have on a small child? How might young children's needs vary in relation to change and separation?

....

C.5.5.c   Try to remember a favourite object from your early childhood. List your memories about your favourite object and your feelings surrounding it.

....

List some of the transitional objects children have brought with them to your workplace/setting.

....

 ### C.5.5.d, C.5.5.e, C.5.5.f, C.5.5.g, C.5.5.h Portfolio Activity

See C.5.4.b on page 76.

C.5.5.i   See C.5.3.k on page 74.

C.5.6 Help children to develop a positive self-image and identity

	Criteria	Knowledge evidence	Date completed
PROGRESS CHECKLIST	C.5.6.a	Knowledge of the development of self-image and identity in young children 6 weeks to 8 years.	
	C.5.6.b	The special needs with regard to identity development of black and ethnic minority children in a predominantly white society.	
	C.5.6.c	The difficulties which may be experienced by children with special needs, abused children and those who are HIV positive in developing a positive self-image and identity.	
	C.5.6.d	The special needs that bilingual children may have with regard to identity.	
	C.5.6.e	Methods of showing approval for children's efforts and why this is important for a child's self-image.	
	C.5.6.f	The planning, provision and evaluation of activities and experiences which explore issues of self-image and identity in accordance with appropriate developmental levels.	
	C.5.6.g	The importance of selecting and providing materials and resources which promote positive and non-stereotypical views of children and adults and provide positive role models.	
	C.5.6.h	Strategies for the promotion among colleagues and other adults including parents of the realisation of the importance of a non-stereotypical view of children and adults.	
	C.5.6.i	A variety of techniques and resources to encourage active exploration among children of different roles and identities in their play.	

C.5.6.j	The importance of discussion, planned and incidental, of gender, race, culture, religion and disability, in the promotion of positive identity.	
C.5.6.k	Patterns of behaviour in young children which may be symptomatic of poor self-image or disturbed identity and when and to whom appropriate referral should be made.	
C.5.6.1	The roles of professional workers to whom candidate can refer children for specialist advice and/or treatment e.g. senior colleague, social worker, educational psychologist, clinical psychologist.	

USEFUL BOOKS

Highlight No 109 The Children Act 1989 and Disability. National Children's Bureau (1992).
Bilingualism in the Primary School. Richard W. Mills and Jean Mills (1993) Routledge.
From Birth to Five Years. M. Sheridan (1987) NFER Nelson.
Building Self-Esteem in Children. Patricia H. Berne and Louis M. Savary (1993).
Childcare: Concerns and Conflicts. S. Morgan and P. Righton (1989) Hodder and Stoughton.

PORTFOLIO ACTIVITY SUMMARY

Criteria	Portfolio page reference	0–1	1–4	4–7
C.5.6.a	See below for Portfolio Activity			
C.5.6.c	See page 81 for Portfolio Activity			
C.5.6.d	See page 81 for Portfolio Activity			
C.5.6.f	See page 81 for Portfolio Activity			
C.5.6.g	See page 81 for Portfolio Activity			
C.5.6.1	See page 82 for Portfolio Activity			

C.5.6.a Portfolio Activity

Present a range of child observations which illustrate different stages of self-image and identity in young children 6 weeks to 8 years. Evaluate and compare your observations, listing the differences you have noticed.

C.5.6.b   See C.5.3.f on page 73.

C.5.6.c Portfolio Activity

Think about the difficulties which may be experienced by children with special needs, abused children and those who are HIV positive in developing a positive self-image. Devise three worksheets or activities, if more appropriate, that would encourage these children to begin to develop a positive self-image.

C.5.6.d Portfolio Activity

In your workplace/setting, where possible, set up a play activity that would meet the specific needs that bilingual children may have in regard to identity. Try to ensure that all their cultural needs are met.

C.5.6.e   Suggest three methods of showing approval for children's efforts.

....

Why is this important for a child's self-image?

....

Why does praising children for effort encourage a positive self-image more than praising for achievement?

....

C.5.6.f Portfolio Activity

See C.5.2.a on page 70.

C.5.6.g Portfolio Activity

Choose two pieces of equipment/resources which promote positive and non-stereotypical views of children and provide positive role models. Compare the equipment and write a review of your findings.

C.5.6.h   What strategies could you use to promote equal opportunities with:

(*a*) colleagues?

....

(*b*) parents?

....

(*c*) other adults?

....

C.5.6.i   Describe two resources that would encourage active exploration among children who have different roles and identities in their play.

....

Suggest a drama technique that might help you to do this more successfully.

....

C.5.6.j   Describe how you would challenge a racist or sexist remark made by a child to another child.

....

C.5.6.k   Think about children who display patterns of behaviour which may be symptomatic of poor self-image or disturbed identity. When and to whom should appropriate referral be made?

....

C.5.6.1 Portfolio Activity

Research the roles of professional workers to whom you can refer children for specialist advice and treatment.

C.7 PROVIDE FOR THE MANAGEMENT OF CHILDREN'S BEHAVIOUR
UNIT WIDE KNOWLEDGE

Criteria	Unit wide knowledge	Date completed
C.7.a	Ways in which the candidate can contribute positively and negatively to children's behaviour.	
C.7.b	Basic knowledge of children's development 6 weeks to 8 years and how this affects their behaviour.	
C.7.c	Key indicators of development and problem behaviour. Emotional, physical, intellectual, social, language.	
C.7.d	Understand that there could be a variety of possible reasons for delayed and regressive behaviour.	
C.7.e	The importance of the causes and antecedents of behaviour, learned or environmental.	
C.7.f	Norms and expectations of behaviour as influenced by class, culture, religion, race, age in both simple/complex behaviours.	
C.7.g	Methods and techniques for verbal and non-verbal communication with adults and children and reasons for use.	
C.7.h	Own role in the setting, the roles of other workers and the liaison between other professional groups.	

Useful books

Babies and Young Children Book 2 – Work and Care. M. Beaver *et al.* (1995) Stanley Thornes.
Caring for the Under 8s – Working to Achieve Good Practice. Jennie and Lance Linden (1993)
Macmillan.

 # Grid C.7

Please tick box when activity is complete.
P = *Portfolio Activity*

C.7.a	C.7.1.b	C.7.2.c	C.7.3.c
		P	

C.7.b	C.7.1.a	C.7.4.f
		P

C.7.c	C.7.4.h	C.7.4.e
		P

C.7.d	C.7.4.d	C.7.4.a
	P	

C.7.e	C.7.3.a	C.7.4.b

C.7.f	C.7.2.a
	P

C.7.g	C.7.2.b	C.7.4.g	C.7.4.c	C.7.3.e	C.7.3.b	C.7.3.f
			P	P		

C.7.h	C.7.3.g	C.7.4.c	C.7.3.d

PORTFOLIO ACTIVITY SUMMARY				
Criteria	**Portfolio page reference**	**0–1**	**1–4**	**4–7**
C.7.a	See page 90 for Portfolio Activity			
C.7.b	See page 100 for Portfolio Activity			
C.7.c	See page 100 for Portfolio Activity			
C.7.d	See page 100 for Portfolio Activity			
C.7.f	See page 88 for Portfolio Activity			
C.7.g	See pages 94 and 100 for Portfolio Activities			

C.7 Provide for the management of children's behaviour

C.7.a, C.7.b, C.7.c, C.7.d, C.7.f, C.7.g – See grid C.7 for cross-referenced knowledge evidence activities.

C.7.1 Contribute to a framework for children's behaviour

<table>
<tr><td rowspan="3" style="background:black;color:white">PROGRESS CHECKLIST</td><td>**Criteria**</td><td>**Knowledge evidence**</td><td>**Date completed**</td></tr>
<tr><td>C.7.1.a</td><td>The limitations of children's memory and understanding and how this may affect their ability to comply with goals and boundaries for behaviour.</td><td></td></tr>
<tr><td>C.7.1.b</td><td>The reasons why frameworks for children's behaviour are necessary.</td><td></td></tr>
</table>

USEFUL BOOKS

Caring for the Under 8s. Jennie and Lance Linden (1993) Macmillan.
Babies and Young Children Book 2 – Work and Care. M. Beaver *et al.* (1995) Stanley Thornes.

C.7.1.a   Scenario: It is lunch time in the Happy Valley Day Care Centre. Natasha (3yrs 2mths) screams 'No!' her mouth open wide. Natasha then leans over her high chair ready to bite Scott.

Scott (2yrs 4mths) has just grabbed a handful of beans from Natasha's plate. Mr Banks reaches out with his hand putting it between Natasha's mouth and Scott's arm. Natasha looks up at Mr Banks who looks down at Natasha. 'That was good stopping when you did. I know you do not like it when someone takes your things. So, Natasha, let me hear you tell Scott not to take your beans.'

Natasha looks at Scott. 'They're mine!' she shouts. Mr Banks responds to Natasha. 'You see, you can talk to people when you are angry but you do not have to bite them because that hurts Scott.' Natasha looks at Scott again. 'My beans.' Scott puts the beans down.

How do you think Natasha felt when Scott grabbed for her food?

....

What are the implications for Natasha's perceptions of acceptable behaviour, and therefore socially acceptable rules within society?

....

How did Mr Banks help Natasha express her feelings in a positive way?

....

C.7.1.b   Scenario: Ben is a very active four-year-old who is playing outside in the nursery garden. Ben has already established himself as the leader of his peer group. Ben has collected some pine cones that are around the edge of the fence and begins to throw them at other children, laughing excitedly with his peer group as they hit the children playing nearby. Ms Hale walks over to Ben, bends down to his level and looks at Ben. 'Well, Ben, you are learning to throw well but if you hit someone with a pine cone they might get hurt or angry.' Ms Hale then asks the group of children, 'Now where can Ben practise throwing safely?' The children begin to look around the nursery garden. 'I know!' Ben shouts in a loud boisterous voice. He points to the grass. 'Over there on the grass.' Ms Hale nods her head in approval, 'Yes, that's a good place, there are no children over there.' Ben, helped by the rest of the children, picks up the pine cones and walks over to the grass area. Ms Hale watches the group for a few minutes, then moves over to the slide area to play with the other children.

Why did Ben need a framework for behaviour?

....

Did Ms Hale intervene in an appropriate way which would have been understood by the children?

....

How would you help Ben and his peer group understand the need for acceptable behaviour, and introduce the rules and boundaries for behaviour?

....

C.7.2 *Promote positive aspects of children's behaviour*

<table>
<tr><td rowspan="4" style="background:black;color:white;">PROGRESS CHECKLIST</td><td>Criteria</td><td>Knowledge evidence</td><td>Date completed</td></tr>
<tr><td>C.7.2.a</td><td>The concept of socially acceptable/desirable behaviour and how this may vary across settings and cultures.</td><td></td></tr>
<tr><td>C.7.2.b</td><td>The basic principles of behaviour modification and why it is important actively to promote positive aspects of behaviour.</td><td></td></tr>
<tr><td>C.7.2.c</td><td>The rationale behind offering explanations and discussion of socially desirable behaviour to children.</td><td></td></tr>
</table>

USEFUL BOOKS

Confident Children. Gael Lindenfield (1994) Thorsons.
Building Self-Esteem in Children. P. H. Berne and L. M. Savary (1993) Continuum Publishing, U.S.
An Introduction to Child Development, 2nd edition. G. C. Davenport (1994) Collins Educational.
Caring for the Under 8s. Jennie and Lance Linden (1993) Macmillan.

PORTFOLIO ACTIVITY SUMMARY

Criteria	Portfolio page reference	0–1	1–4	4–7
C.7.2.a	See below for Portfolio Activity			
C.7.2.c	See page 90 for Portfolio Activity			

C.7.2.a *Portfolio Activity*

Definition of **socially acceptable behaviour***:*

Behaviour that is accepted and rewarded by the society in which you live i.e. the norms of the society.

> *(a) In terms of cultural identity how can the socially acceptable behaviour of a child differ?*

(b) *Design five menu plans that are reflective of children living in a multi-cultural society. Each individual menu plan should include four meals that cater for each child's cultural identity.*

(c) *Children's behaviour needs to be understood in line with the child's individual developmental context. Therefore a child demonstrating unacceptable behaviour in one environment may not show the same behaviour in a different environment. Likewise, unacceptable behaviour may not be shown when with one particular adult but occurs when in the company of a different adult.*

From the following identify possible reasons why a child's behaviour might change according to the setting/culture they experience.

(1) *The home setting but not at nursery/school.*
(2) *Within nursery/school but not in the home setting.*
(3) *Both the home setting and nursery/school.*

C.7.2.b   Record an account of the basic principles on which behaviour modification is founded.

....

Explain the importance of active positive reinforcement.

....

What is meant by the term 'behaviour shaping' in accordance with Skinner's theory?

....

C.7.2.c Portfolio Activity

From the diagram on page 90 record an individual account of how the aspects that determine a child's behaviour can also influence socially desirable behaviour both in positive and negative ways.

Then discuss why it is important for the carer to explain to a child the need for socially acceptable behaviour.

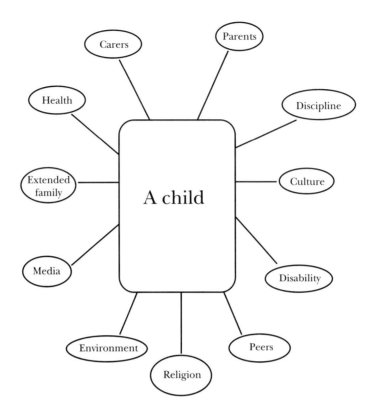

C.7.3 Manage unwanted aspects of children's behaviour

PROGRESS CHECKLIST	Criteria	Knowledge evidence	Date completed
	C.7.3.a	The factors and circumstances which may encourage or provoke children to display difficult or negative behaviour.	
	C.7.3.b	The reasons why a calm and controlled manner is important and why physical punishment is not necessary, acceptable or effective.	
	C.7.3.c	The basic principles of behaviour modification and how they can be used to manage children's unwanted behaviour.	
	C.7.3.d	The importance of boundary setting and consistency of application by significant adults.	
	C.7.3.e	Principles for selecting reward system to be used when dealing with problem behaviour.	
	C.7.3.f	Techniques of physical and non-physical control.	
	C.7.3.g	Legal implications of physical control and/or methods of control.	

USEFUL BOOKS

Assertive Discipline. Lee Carter and Marlene Carter.
Children First. Penelope Leach (1994) Penguin.
Caring for Children. Kate Williams and Ruth Gardner (1994) Pitman.
The Language of Discipline. Bill Rogers (1994) Resources in Education.
Good Habits, Bad Habits. Dr John Pearce (1994) Thorsons.
Bad Behaviour Tantrums and Tempers. Dr John Pearce (1993) Thorsons.

PORTFOLIO ACTIVITY SUMMARY

Criteria	Portfolio page reference	0–1	1–4	4–7
C.7.3.d	See page 93 for Portfolio Activity			
C.7.3.e	See page 94 for Portfolio Activity			
C.7.3.g	See page 96 for Portfolio Activity			

C.7.3.a   Give three reasons why a child's behaviour may regress.

....

Give three reasons why a child may use aggressive behaviour.

....

Give three reasons why a child may use language that is offensive.

....

Describe how the care giver could help a child to overcome one of these behaviours.

....

Using the following headings, describe what you feel would be appropriate to investigate in relation to a child's anti-social behaviour:

(*a*) emotional environment at home;
(*b*) family history;
(*c*) child's individual history.

....

C.7.3.b   Bearing in mind that children imitate and learn from the way that people around them behave, discuss why adults must use a calm and controlled manner when dealing with problem behaviour.

....

Record a detailed account suggesting reasons why physical punishment is not necessarily an acceptable or effective outcome in seeking to change a child's unacceptable or challenging behaviour.

....

C.7.3.c   Scenario: Leroy is a four-year-old boy attending reception class in a school situated in a newly developed housing estate. Leroy is an only child who has very caring and rather over-protective parents, who also have high expectations for Leroy. There are 21 children in Leroy's class, along with the teacher and two nursery nurses. Leroy is not used to coping with the rough and tumble of large groups of children and is used to the individual attention of his parents. Lately, Leroy has become increasingly angry and also gets very upset at having to share things and wait his turn. Leroy insists on being at the front of the line at play time and pushes Vincent, one of the other children, out of his way causing him to tumble and cut his knee.

Describe the way in which you could use a behaviour modification approach to resolve the child's behaviour.

....

What action would you then take in this situation?

....

Explain the stages of your actions and why you chose them.

....

Discuss how you might suggest to the child's parents ways in which they could encourage their child to be more socially mobile.

....

Draw up a chart to record behaviour and that could be used to monitor behaviour.

....

C.7.3.d   Why is it important to clearly distinguish boundaries for children?

....

Why is consistency important?

....

 ### C.7.3.d Portfolio Activity

Draw up a list of rules that explain to children the discipline used in the workplace/setting, and set the boundaries within the following:

> *(a) day care provision;*
> *(b) reception class infant school;*
> *(c) family placement.*

Discuss the advantages and disadvantages of modified assertive discipline.

C.7.3.e   When using a reward, or sanction with a child, discuss the importance of implementing the reward or sanction immediately following the behaviour change.

....

Draw up a definition of reward that you could use with a group of children. State the age of the children it would be used with.

....

Give examples of two uses of rewards. Describe the situation you would use them in, and how long they would be used for. Also, why you are using them, and what you consider will be the outcome of the use of these rewards.

....

 ### *C.7.3.e Portfolio Activity*

Draw up an example of an illustrated behaviour chart that can be completed by the child and which details the reward involved.

C.7.3.f   Types of Physical and Non-Physical Control:

use of body language and gestures   sending to bed
smacking   defining boundaries
shouting   isolation
pinching   restraining
threatening   locking in dark
punching   being quiet
swearing   distractors
channelling

From the list above draw up a table of physical and non-physical control like the one shown here.

Physical	Non-physical

Describe how you would attempt to control a child who is using challenging behaviour by use of non-physical techniques.

....

Describe one way you could safely and physically restrain a child, taking into consideration the legal aspects involved.

....

C.7.3.g Portfolio Activity

Read the following in relation to the tasks:

> 6.2.1   *People responsible for running a day care facility need to have an agreed policy on its day-to-day operation and to develop procedures for modifying unacceptable behaviour in the children which will include appropriate sanctions. It will encourage development of a sense of right and wrong behaviour if children are encouraged to co-operate in the social organisation of the facility. The sanctions applied in the case of unacceptable behaviour must take account of the age and stage of development of the child, be given at the time, be relevant to the action or actions, and be fair. The child should always be told why his behaviour is not acceptable and the reasons for applying a particular sanction. Providers and childminders should ensure that parents are fully informed about and support the policy on modifying unacceptable behaviour and the range of sanctions.*

> 6.2.2   *Corporal punishment (smacking, slapping or shaking) is illegal in maintained schools and should not be used by any other parties within the scope of this guidance. It is permissible to take necessary physical action in an emergency to prevent personal injury either to the child, other children or an adult or serious damage to property.*

> **Source:** *The Children's Act 1989 Guidance and Regulation Vol. 2, HMSO 1991*

Discuss the implications for the carer in the work setting.

You have been asked to give a short talk to a group of parents on the reasons for developing self-discipline with children within your work setting. You need to refer to the legal requirements, but also wish to emphasise that physical punishment of any form does not work.

(a)   Prepare your talk in written format.

(b)   When your talk has been prepared, tape record it, emphasising points you feel are important. Pay particular attention to your voice tone, and what you are saying. Remember you need to support your argument against physical punishment of any form and the need for children to learn socially acceptable behaviour by positive examples.

C.7.4 Respond to persistent problem behaviour

	Criteria	Knowledge evidence	Date completed
PROGRESS CHECKLIST	C.7.4.a	The factors and circumstances which may support or provoke changes in the usual behaviour pattern of young children.	
	C.7.4.b	The concepts and behavioural signs of regression, withdrawal, attention-seeking, anti-social behaviour and self-damaging behaviour.	
	C.7.4.c	Sources of specialist advice and guidance and how to gain access to them.	
	C.7.4.d	The role played by additives and chemicals in food and drink.	
	C.7.4.e	The principles of constructing a recording system for children's behaviour.	
	C.7.4.f	The need to discriminate between relevant and irrelevant information in relation to behaviours needing attention.	
	C.7.4.g	Simple techniques for behaviour modification, including positive reinforcement and time out.	
	C.7.4.h	Techniques for observing and monitoring children's behaviour individually and in groups.	

USEFUL BOOKS

Dictionary of Social Work. Martin Thomas and John Pieron (1995) HarperCollins.
Worries and Fears. Dr John Pearce (1989) Thorsons.
Fighting, Teasing and Bullying. Dr John Pearce (1989) HarperCollins.
Behaviour Problems in Young Children. Jo Douglas (1985) Routledge.
Children First. Penelope Leach (1994) Penguin.

PORTFOLIO ACTIVITY SUMMARY

Criteria	Portfolio page reference	0–1	1–4	4–7
C.7.4.c	See page 100 for Portfolio Activity			
C.7.4.d	See page 100 for Portfolio Activity			
C.7.4.e–f	See page 100 for Portfolio Activity			

C.7.4.a   Study the following diagram, then choose one aspect from the diagram and give a brief overview.

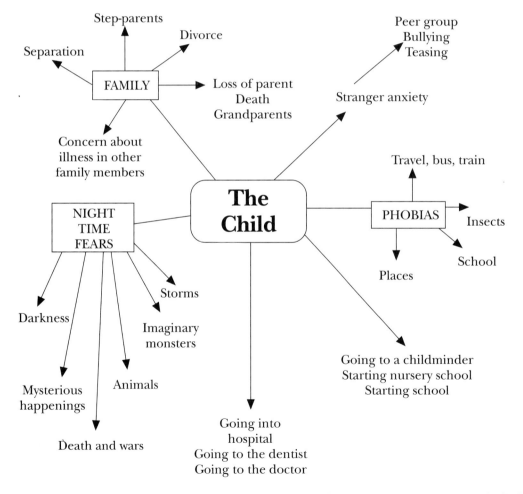

Discuss any factors that would help to contribute to and support your belief that a child's behaviour was causing concern in relation to the chosen aspect.

....

Record the behaviour that a child would demonstrate and how it is associated to the chosen aspect.

....

Record factors that would help to contribute and support any programme of behaviour modification.

....

C.7.4.b   Draw up a table like the one below and allocate the behaviours listed to the appropriate headings:

a child holding his or her breath
bed wetting
acting up in peer group
requesting help with feeding/dressing
refusing to speak
spitting
biting others
temper outburst
refusal to take part in anything
biting themselves
refusing to eat

screaming
writing/drawing reverts to early
    stage/age
hitting others
wanting to be held constantly
interrupting conversations
reverting to baby talk
self-mutilation
isolating themselves
head banging

Regression	Withdrawal	Attention-seeking behaviour

Anti-social behaviour	Self-damaging behaviour

Describe the difference between attention-seeking behaviour and that of anti-social behaviour, giving examples to support your explanations.

....

What would be some of the common behaviour symptoms of a child under stress?

....

C.7.4.c   List five specialists who would be involved with a child with behaviour problems and state who refers them.

....

C.7.4.c Portfolio Activity

Research two of these specialists, their role and involvement with a child.

C.7.4.d   Describe three types of food that can have an adverse effect on children's behaviour, giving an explanation of how and why they affect behaviour.

....

C.7.4.d Portfolio Activity

You have been asked to draw up a 'shopping list' of the types of foods and drinks that are known to have an effect on children's behaviour. Your shopping list will be used for a poster to be displayed in the entrance of the nursery to draw parents' attention to those items. With this aim in mind design your shopping list in poster format with illustrations.

C.7.4.e, C.7.4.f Portfolio Activity

Referring back to task C.7.4.a, using one aspect of regressive behaviour, draw up a suitable recording system to monitor the behaviour.

State why you have chosen to use your recording system, the appropriateness in association to behaviour chosen, how and when it will be used, length of time etc.

Discuss and describe how you would inform all of the people involved in your recording, referring to the specific behaviours that would be important to record.

C.7.4.g   Draw a similar table to the one below and write down under the appropriate heading the advantages and disadvantages of behaviour modification.

Advantages	Disadvantages

What is meant by the term 'time out'?

....

How can 'time out' be used to promote positive behaviour?

....

C.7.4.h   For use of techniques in observation refer to unit C.16 'Observe and assess the development and behaviour of children'.

C.10 PROMOTE CHILDREN'S SENSORY AND INTELLECTUAL DEVELOPMENT
UNIT WIDE KNOWLEDGE

	Criteria	Unit wide knowledge	Date completed
PROGRESS CHECKLIST	C.10.a	The course of children's sensory and intellectual development between 6 weeks and 8 years and how this relates to other aspects of their development.	
	C.10.b	The idea of 'milestones' based on normative measurement and a maturational model of development, with awareness of its limitations. Knowledge of developmental scales which use these theories, e.g. Mary Sheridan, and their application in practice. Understanding of the role of these theories in practice.	
	C.10.c	The ideas of sequences/stages, most comprehensively developed by Piaget. It is not necessary to grasp in detail the logical basis of particular stages such as concrete operations, or their individual components. It is important to understand the notion of stages and the consequent notion of readiness as a biological condition as well as a function of prior learning. The use and abuse of these concepts in practice.	
	C.10.d	The idea which comes from many theoretical sources that children actively construct their own world view through using their inbuilt intellectual capacity and the nature of the environments in which they participate. The idea of the child as active learner and the implications for workers.	

C.10.e	The basis and application of learning theory, and its limitations. Useful concepts such as reinforcement and behaviour modification.	
C.10.f	The concept of perception; the different types of perception, visual, auditory, tactile and their role in children's development; how children learn through perception.	
C.10.g	The needs and requirements of young children with respect to sensory and intellectual development and how these might be met.	
C.10.h	How children learn and the ways in which adult interaction can facilitate this learning.	
C.10.i	The possible environmental, physical, social, cultural and genetic factors which can enhance or impair children's sensory and intellectual development.	
C.10.j	The role of assumptions concerned with race and gender in intellectual development.	
C.10.k	The role of other professionals such as class teachers, educational psychologists, speech therapists.	
C.10.l	The particular difficulties which may affect the sensory and intellectual development of children who use more than one language.	
C.10.m	How children's special needs might affect their sensory and intellectual development.	

USEFUL BOOKS

Babies and Young Children Book 1 – Development 0–7. M. Beaver *et al.* (1994) Stanley Thornes.
Special Issues in Child Care. M. O'Hagan and M. Smith (1994) Bailliere Tindall.
Special Educational Needs. ed. R. Gulliford and G. Upton (1992) Routledge.
From Birth to Five Years. M. Sheridan (1987) NFER Nelson.
A Practical Guide to Child Observation. C. Hobart and J. Frankel (1994) Stanley Thornes.
Profiling, Recording and Observing – A resource pack for the early years. B. Steiner *et al.* (1993) Routledge.

✓ Grid C.10

Please tick box when activity is complete.

P = *Portfolio Activity*

C.10.a	C.10.3.b
	P

C.10.c	C.10.1.a
	P

C.10.d	C.10.3.d	C.10.3.e	C.10.4.a	C.10.4.d	C.10.4.e	C.10.4.f	C.10.4.g	C.10.4.h
	P	P		P	P	P	P	P

C.10.f	C.10.2.a	C.10.2.b

C.10.g	C.10.1.c	C.10.2.e	C.10.2.f
		P	P

C.10.h	C.10.1.b	C.10.1.d	C.10.1.f	C.10.3.c
	P	P		P

C.10.i	C.10.1.e	C.10.1.g	C.10.4.c

C.10.j	C.10.4.i
	P

C.10.k	C.10.2.d
	P

C.10.m	C.10.2.c	C.10.4.b	C.10.3.a	C.10.4.j
		P	P	

PORTFOLIO ACTIVITY SUMMARY

Criteria	Portfolio page reference	0–1	1–4	4–7
C.10.a	See page 114 for Portfolio Activity			
C.10.b	See page 106 for Portfolio Activity			
C.10.c	See page 108 for Portfolio Activity			
C.10.d	See pages 115 and 118 for Portfolio Activities			
C.10.e	See page 106 for Portfolio Activity			
C.10.g	See page 112 for Portfolio Activity			
C.10.h	See pages 108 and 114 for Portfolio Activities			
C.10.j	See page 118 for Portfolio Activity			
C.10.k	See page 111 for Portfolio Activity			
C.10.l	See page 106 for Portfolio Activity			
C.10.m	See pages 114 and 117 for Portfolio Activities			

C.10 Promote children's sensory and intellectual development

C.10.a – See grid C.10 for cross-referenced knowledge evidence activities.

C.10.b Portfolio Activity

Do a group observation of children of the same age. Record a language activity (using an audio cassette recorder, if possible) and do a comparison of the children's language and cognitive development, taking into account the idea of milestones.

What are the possible disadvantages of using an age/stage model of development when observing and evaluating the progress of young children?

C.10.c, C.10.d – See grid C.10 for cross-referenced knowledge evidence activities.

C.10.e Portfolio Activity

Basic who's who in psychology:

The psychologists – Sigmund Freud
Jean Piaget
Lev Semyonovich Vygotsky

The behaviourists – Ivan Pavlov
B. F. Skinner

Choose one *of the above. Outline the advantages/disadvantages of one aspect of their work in relation to children's intellectual development.*

C.10.f, C.10.g, C.10.h, C.10.i, C.10.j, C.10.k – See grid C.10 for cross-referenced knowledge evidence activities.

C.10.l Portfolio Activity

Investigate the languages used by the children in your workplace/placement.

How many languages are spoken by the children and staff? Which languages are spoken?

Are there children who are bilingual or multilingual? When do they use languages other than English?

What kind of support is available locally for children whose first language is not English?

C.10.m – See grid C.10 for cross-referenced knowledge evidence activities.

C.10.1 Help children to develop their attention span and memory

	Criteria	Knowledge evidence	Date completed
PROGRESS CHECKLIST	C.10.1.a	The sequence and processes of intellectual development between 6 weeks and 8 years.	
	C.10.1.b	A variety of appropriate experiences designed to promote intellectual development, their potential value and how to provide them.	
	C.10.1.c	How to extend experiences and learning through awareness of an individual child or group of children's broad level of development.	
	C.10.1.d	The role that attention and memory play in learning.	
	C.10.1.e	The needs of individual children in the group and the possible reasons for low concentration and attention.	
	C.10.1.f	How to provide appropriate experiences to extend memory and recall.	
	C.10.1.g	The limitations of memory and concentration in young children, and factors affecting this.	

USEFUL BOOKS

From Birth to Five Years. M. Sheridan (1987) NFER Nelson.
Children's Minds. M. Donaldson (1978) Fontana.
Babies and Young Children Book 1 – Development 0–7. M. Beaver *et al.* (1994) Stanley Thornes.
Special Issues in Child Care. M. O'Hagan and M. Smith (1994) Bailliere Tindall.

PORTFOLIO ACTIVITY SUMMARY		0–1	1–4	4–7
Criteria	**Portfolio page reference**			
C.10.1.a	See below for Portfolio Activity			
C.10.1.b	See below for Portfolio Activity			
C.10.1.d, f	See below for Portfolio Activity			

C.10.1.a Portfolio Activity

Find out about Piaget's theories and stages of cognitive development.

Make a chart showing Piaget's view of children's cognitive development.

Do the conservation of mass experiment, using play dough, with a young child at your workplace/placement. Record your results. Evaluate/compare with Piaget's results.

*(**Adapted from** Babies and Young Children. . . . M. Beaver et al. pp. 143–4)*

C.10.1.b Portfolio Activity

Describe two activities which you have provided for young children. How did each activity promote the children's intellectual development?

C.10.1.c   Describe appropriate experiences that promote the language development of a child or children for each of the following age ranges:

(*a*) 0–12 months;

....

(*b*) 1–4 years;

....

(*c*) 4–7 years.

....

C.10.1.d, C.10.1.f Portfolio Activity

Design a memory game for a young child. Specify the age of the child, the learning outcomes for the child and how the game was made.

Use the game with a young child. Evaluate the child's responses to the game and suggest any modifications.

C.10.1.e   Give possible reasons for low concentration and attention in young children.

....

C.10.1.g   List four factors which may impair children's sensory and intellectual development.

....

C.10.2 Help children to develop awareness and understanding of sensory experiences

	Criteria	Knowledge evidence	Date completed
PROGRESS CHECKLIST	C.10.2.a	The sequences and processes of sensory development.	
	C.10.2.b	What sensory experiences are, their value and how to provide appropriate sensory experiences.	
	C.10.2.c	The concept of sensory impairment, its practical implications for children and for workers promoting their development.	
	C.10.2.d	When and how children might be referred for assessment of sensory functions.	
	C.10.2.e	How to provide a safe and stimulating environment to encourage children's sensory development.	
	C.10.2.f	A variety of appropriate materials and equipment to encourage children's sensory development.	

USEFUL BOOKS

Children with Special Needs – A Guide for Parents and Carers. R. Woolfson (1991) Faber and Faber.
Special Educational Needs. ed. R. Gulliford and G. Upton (1992) Routledge.
Babies and Young Children Book 1 – Development 0–7. M. Beaver *et al.* (1994) Stanley Thornes.
Play with a Purpose for the Under Sevens. E. Matterson (1989) Penguin.
Bright Ideas in the Early Years – Learning Through Play. J. Morris and L. Mort (1991) Scholastic.
Meeting Special Needs in Ordinary Schools. S. Hegarty (1993) Cassell (Chapter 8).

PORTFOLIO ACTIVITY SUMMARY

Criteria	Portfolio page reference	0–1	1–4	4–7
C.10.2.d	See below for Portfolio Activity			
C.10.2.e, f	See page 112 for Portfolio Activity			

C.10.2.a,   Find out about young children's sensory and perceptual development.
C.10.2.b   Give an example activity to develop each of the following:

(*a*) sensory skills at

9 months;
2 years;
4 years.

....

(*b*) perceptual skills at

9 months;
2 years;
4 years.

....

C.10.2.c   State two practical ways to promote the sensory and intellectual development of:

(*a*) a child with a hearing impairment;

....

(*b*) a child with a visual impairment.

....

C.10.2.d Portfolio Activity

There are many agencies which may be involved in meeting the needs of a child whose language development is delayed. For example, health visitor, speech therapist, portage worker, language unit, nursery, individual classroom support, charities, local initiatives.

Find out about one of the above agencies.

Compile a fact sheet using the information you have gained.

C.10.2.e, C.10.2.f Portfolio Activity

Using the information gained from doing activity C.10.2a, b (about children's sensory and perceptual development) and your own experiences in the workplace/placement, design a stimulating play environment within the following age ranges:

    (a) 0–12 months;
    (b) 1–4 years;
    (c) 4–7 years.

Specify the exact age group, include information on the appropriate materials and equipment to encourage the children's sensory development and which skills are to be developed.

Draw a plan of the play area and provide a short written account of your design ideas.

C.10.3 Help children to understand basic concepts

	Criteria	Knowledge evidence	Date completed
PROGRESS CHECKLIST	C.10.3.a	The types of concepts in the range and why some may be difficult for children to understand.	
	C.10.3.b	The usual sequence of intellectual and language development and how this is linked to the acquisition of basic concepts.	
	C.10.3.c	How children learn/acquire basic concepts and how their understanding of concepts may change over time.	
	C.10.3.d	How observation, discovery and exploratory learning can be used in developing children's understanding of the natural and physical world.	
	C.10.3.e	The role of play in conceptual development.	

USEFUL BOOKS

Children's Concepts and the Primary Curriculum. C. J. Willig (1990) Paul Chapman.
Understanding Your Child – A Parent's Guide to Child Psychology. R. Woolfson (1989) Faber and Faber. (Chapter 15: Language Development; also Developmental Checklists at the end of the book.)
Children with Special Needs – A Guide for Parents and Carers. R. Woolfson (1991) Faber and Faber.
Children with Special Needs. H. Chasty and J. Friel (1991) Jessica Kingsley.
Signposts to Special Needs. National Children's Bureau (1991) NES Arnold.
Babies and Young Children Book 1 – Development 0–7. M. Beaver *et al.* (1994) Stanley Thornes.
Special Issues in Child Care. M. O'Hagan and M. Smith (1994) Bailliere Tindall.

PORTFOLIO ACTIVITY SUMMARY				
Criteria	Portfolio page reference	0–1	1–4	4–7
C.10.3.a	See below for Portfolio Activity			
C.10.3.b	See below for Portfolio Activity			
C.10.3.c	See below for Portfolio Activity			
C.10.3.d	See page 115 for Portfolio Activity			
C.10.3.e	See page 115 for Portfolio Activity			

C.10.3.a Portfolio Activity

Find out why some children may have difficulties understanding certain concepts, e.g. children with specific learning difficulties such as dyslexia.

Write a short report on your findings.

C.10.3.b Portfolio Activity

Read about the Nature vs Nurture debate, in terms of a child's intellectual development, in Babies and Young Children Book 1 – Development 0–7 *and* Special Issues in Child Care.

Decide for yourself what you think is the combination of nature and nurture in children's language development. Give reasons for your answer.

C.10.3.c Portfolio Activity

Draw a picture or diagram that represents the different kinds of learning that you have experienced yourself – either as an adult or as a child.

Use your picture to show all the different ways in which you learn and have learned.

Now think about one or two of the children with whom you work. Can you see any evidence in them of these different kinds of learning? What sorts of pathways and patterns can you see in their learning as you watch them play and interact with you and their peers?

Draw a spidergram or similar chart to record the ways children learn at your workplace/placement.

*(**Adapted from** Making Assessment Work, Drummond et al. (1994) NFER Nelson)*

C.10.3.d Portfolio Activity

Find out how children develop their powers of observation and visual memory, and how adults can help them to do this.

Design an activity card to encourage children's observation skills and visual memory; indicate which age group the activity is for.

Use the activity card with a child or group of children; evaluate their responses and suggest any modifications.

C.10.3.e Portfolio Activity

Devise a play activity for a young child within each of the following age ranges:

       (a) 0–12 months;
       (b) 1–4 years;
       (c) 4–7 years.

Specify the age/stage appropriateness in relation to the child's conceptual development and the learning outcomes for the child.

Use the activity with the child and evaluate the responses of the child, how the activity was implemented and any modifications.

C.10.4 Help children to express their imagination and creativity

	Criteria	Knowledge evidence	Date completed
PROGRESS CHECKLIST	C.10.4.a	The role and value of self-expression and creativity in children's sensory and intellectual development.	
	C.10.4.b	Why some children have difficulty or are reluctant to participate in imaginative and creative activities and ways of encouraging children to express themselves freely.	
	C.10.4.c	The importance of creating a safe and stimulating environment where children can express themselves freely.	
	C.10.4.d	The sorts of materials and equipment which may help children to express creativity and imagination and the rationale behind their use.	
	C.10.4.e	The role of fantasy and imaginative play in children's sensory and intellectual development.	
	C.10.4.f	The relative significance of process and product in children's creativity.	
	C.10.4.g	Ways of supporting children's spontaneous imaginative play.	
	C.10.4.h	When and how sensitive adult intervention is needed to help extend and develop children's imaginative play and awareness of the disruptive potential of such intervention.	
	C.10.4.i	How children's expression can be constrained or conditioned by gender or other stereotypical roles and how to counteract this.	
	C.10.4.j	How to adapt equipment and activities as necessary to make it easier for children with special needs to express their creativity and imagination.	

USEFUL BOOKS

Signposts to Special Needs. National Children's Bureau (1991) NES Arnold.
Bilingualism in the Primary School. ed. R. W. Mills and J. Mills (1993) Routledge.
A Practical Guide to Child Observation. C. Hobart and J. Frankel (1994) Stanley Thornes.
Creative Play. D. Einon (1986) Penguin.

PORTFOLIO ACTIVITY SUMMARY				
Criteria	**Portfolio page reference**	**0–1**	**1–4**	**4–7**
C.10.4.b	See below for Portfolio Activity			
C.10.4.d, e, f, g, h	See page 118 for Portfolio Activity			
C.10.4.i	See page 118 for Portfolio Activity			

C.10.4.a   Describe an activity which promotes *active learning* for each of the following:

(*a*) yourself as a learner;

....

(b) a child at your workplace/placement.

....

C.10.4.b Portfolio Activity

Devise an activity which encourages a group of children to express themselves freely in an imaginative or creative way.

Specify the age range suitability, how the activity could be implemented and learning outcomes for the children.

If possible, implement the activity and evaluate the children's actions and responses. Suggest any possible modifications to the activity, for example, changes to suit different children's needs, a different age group or children with special needs.

C.10.4.c   List four factors which may enhance children's sensory and intellectual development.

....

C.10.4.d, C.10.4.e, C.10.4.f, C.10.4.g, C.10.4.h Portfolio Activity

Carry out an observation of a child during an imaginative or creative play activity.

Make notes on, and evaluate the child's intellectual development.

Suggest ways to extend and develop the child's imaginative play.

Include information on the use of any appropriate materials and equipment plus the role of the adult in developing this type of activity.

C.10.4.i Portfolio Activity

Devise a role play which illustrates how children's expression can be constrained or conditioned by race or gender stereotypes. The role play must also highlight ways to counteract stereotypical views.

The format of the role play should be that of either a talk show or a press conference; roles included could be host(s)/press secretary, guests/celebrities, audience/reporters. The characters in the role play should have a variety of viewpoints.

If possible, act out your role play with your fellow students/colleagues.

Evaluate the outcome.

C.10.4.j   Adapt a creative activity to enable a child with special needs to participate with a group of children.

C.11 Promote the development of children's language and communication skills

UNIT WIDE KNOWLEDGE

	Criteria	Unit wide knowledge	Date completed
PROGRESS CHECKLIST	C.11.a	Sequence of development of language and communication in children 6 weeks to 8 years and how this relates to other aspects of their development.	
	C.11.b	The needs and requirements of young children with respect to developing their language and communication skills and how these might be met; factors which influence language and communication skills development.	
	C.11.c	The importance of encouraging the child's listening and comprehension skills.	
	C.11.d	Understand the candidate's own role, the role of colleagues and the need for access to other professional workers e.g. speech therapists within, and as appropriate to, the setting.	
	C.11.e	The concept of sensory impairment as it may affect development of language and communication.	
	C.11.f	The common reasons for language delay.	
	C.11.g	The need for development of candidate's own interpersonal skills.	

C.11.h	The value of praise and encouragement in developing children's listening and communication skills.	
C.11.i	The importance of respecting and acknowledging a child's background, culture and religion.	
C.11.j	The basis for and the need to encourage the development of pre-reading and pre-writing skills in young children.	
C.11.k	Current thinking with regard to early reading and writing and their implications for workers with young children.	
C.11.l	The support and encouragement which may be needed by children who use more than one language.	
C.11.m	Children's special needs which may affect the development of their language and communication skills.	

USEFUL BOOKS

Babies and Young Children Book 1 – Development 0–7. Beaver *et al.* (1994) Stanley Thornes.
Language and Learning. J. Britton (1992) Penguin.
An Introduction to Child Development. C. G. Davenport (1994) Collins Educational.
Special Issues in Child Care. M. O'Hagan and M. Smith (1994) Bailliere Tindall.

✓ *Grid C.11*

Please tick box when activity is complete.
P = *Portfolio Activity*

C.11.a	C.11.1.h	C.11.2.c	C.11.2.d	C.11.2.i	C.11.4.d	C.11.5.f	C.11.5.g	C.11.5.i
		P	P	P			P	

C.11.b	C.11.1.b	C.11.1.c	C.11.1.e	C.11.1.g	C.11.2.a	C.11.2.b	C.11.4.a	C.11.5.c	C.11.6.h
	P	P	P	P	P	P	P	P	P

C.11.c	C.11.2.f	C.11.2.h	C.11.2.k	C.11.2.j	C.11.3.a	C.11.3.b	C.11.4.b	C.11.5.b	C.11.6.g
				P	P	P	P	P	P

C.11.d	C.11.1.d	C.11.2.e	C.11.5.d
	P	P	P

C.11.e		C.11.6.i
		P

C.11.f	C.11.4.f	C.11.5.e
	P	P

C.11.g	C.11.4.e

C.11.h	C.11.1.a	C.11.2.g	C.11.3.c	C.11.4.c	C.11.5.a
	P		P	P	P

C.11.i	C.11.1.f	C.11.1.i	C.11.5.h	C.11.6.a

C.11.j	C.11.6.b	C.11.6.c
	P	P

C.11.k	C.11.6.d	C.11.6.e
	P	P

C.11.l	C.11.3.d	C.11.6.f
	P	P

PORTFOLIO ACTIVITY SUMMARY

Criteria	Portfolio page reference	0–1	1–4	4–7
C.11.a	See pages 129 and 138 for Portfolio Activities			
C.11.b	See pages 125 and 141 for Portfolio Activities			
C.11.c	See pages 121, 132, 134 and 137 for Portfolio Activities			
C.11.d	See pages 126 and 129 for Portfolio Activities			
C.11.e	See page 141 for Portfolio Activity			
C.11.f	See page 135 for Portfolio Activity			
C.11.h	See page 132 for Portfolio Activity			
C.11.j	See page 140 for Portfolio Activity			
C.11.k	See page 140 for Portfolio Activity			
C.11.l	See page 132 for Portfolio Activity			

C.11 Promote the development of children's language and communication skills

C.11.a, C.11.b, C.11.c, C.11.d, C.11.e, C.11.f, C.11.g, C.11.h, C.11.i, C.11.j, C.11.k, C.11.l – See grid C.11 for cross-referenced knowledge evidence activities.

C.11.m   How may the following special needs affect a child's language and communication skills?

(*a*) Autism

....

(*b*) Cerebral palsy

....

(*c*) Down's syndrome

....

(*d*) Cleft palate

....

(*e*) Stammer

....

C.11.1 Identify the language and communication abilities of an individual child

	Criteria	Knowledge evidence	Date completed
PROGRESS CHECKLIST	C.11.1.a	The importance of establishing an effective, confident and caring working relationship with the child.	
	C.11.1.b	Communication techniques which encourage children to communicate freely. These may include: active listening (minimum talking by the adult); leaving time for child to talk; careful phrasing of adult response; open-ended questioning.	
	C.11.1.c	Methods of obtaining information regarding children's language and communication abilities. This may include: tape recordings; child observations; use of questioning techniques.	
	C.11.1.d	When and how to call on specialist advice to assist identification of communication abilities.	
	C.11.1.e	The ways of recording relevant information about children's communication abilities.	
	C.11.1.f	The family background and circumstances of the child including the parents' wishes with regard to language development.	
	C.11.1.g	The effects of different settings and environment on the child's expression and communication.	
	C.11.1.h	The variety of ways in which children seek to communicate and how these may support or substitute each other.	
	C.11.1.i	The rules and boundaries of confidentiality within the setting with regard to children's communication abilities and family background.	

USEFUL BOOKS

Language and Learning. J. Britton (1992) Penguin.
Talking and Learning. J. Tough (1985) Ward Lock.
The Education of the Young Child. ed. D. Fontana (1994) Basil Blackwell.
A Practical Guide to Child Observation. C. Hobart and J. Frankel (1994) Stanley Thornes.
Children with Special Needs – A Guide for Parents and Carers. R. Woolfson (1991) Faber and Faber.

PORTFOLIO ACTIVITY SUMMARY

Criteria	Portfolio page reference	0–1	1–4	4–7
C.11.1.a	See page 132 for Portfolio Activity			
C.11.1.b	See below for Portfolio Activity			
C.11.1.c, e, g	See below for Portfolio Activity			
C.11.1.d	See page 126 for Portfolio Activity			

C.11.1.a Portfolio Activity

See C.11.3.c on page 132.

C.11.1.b Portfolio Activity

Devise a language activity which uses a variety of communication techniques, including:

- *active listening;*
- *leaving time for children to talk;*
- *careful phrasing of adult responses;*
- *open-ended questioning.*

C.11.1.c, C.11.1.e, C.11.1.g, C.11.2.a, C.11.2.b, C.11.4.a, C.11.5.c Portfolio Activity

Do two observations.

> *(1) (a)* Observe *a child during a one-to-one language activity with an adult (not yourself).*
>
> *(b)* Comment *on: the child's communication skills, verbal and non-verbal; the child's level of interaction and participation in the activity; the language used by the child* and *the adult, including questioning techniques.*

(2) (c) Observe *a group of children (using a tape recorder) involved in a language game. The child from the first observation should be included in this group.*

(b) Comment *on each child's communication skills, verbal and non-verbal; level of interaction and participation in the game situation; use of language.*

(c) Evaluate *the child who was involved in both observations e.g. any differences in the communication skills and/or language recorded? Any variations in the level of interaction and participation? Suggest reasons why there may be differences.*

 ### C.11.1.d Portfolio Activity

Compile a fact sheet on the role of the speech therapist. Consider the following: access to help and where help takes place e.g. child's home, nursery, school or special unit.

C.11.1.f,   A child who is normally lively and talkative suddenly becomes shy and
C.11.1.i   withdrawn and unwilling to communicate with others in the setting where you
are working.

(*a*) What would you do to help this child?

....

(*b*) How would you inform the parents of your concerns?

....

(*c*) How could you involve the parents in any strategies to encourage the child to communicate freely again?

....

C.11.1.h   Write down three ways a baby communicates at:

(*a*) 0–6 months;

....

(*b*) 6–12 months.

....

What is 'telegraphic' speech?

....

Write out these sentences in telegraphic speech.

(*a*) 'I've fallen off the swing and hurt my knee.'

....

(*b*) 'Shall we go for a walk?'

....

(*c*) 'Let Daddy sit there.'

....

(*d*) 'How long is the train?'

....

(*e*) 'Didn't you have some milk yesterday?'

....

C.11.2 Facilitate communication with a child

	Criteria	Knowledge evidence	Date completed
PROGRESS CHECKLIST	C.11.2.a	A variety of direct and indirect questioning techniques.	
	C.11.2.b	Types of activity which encourage children to communicate one-to-one with adults.	
	C.11.2.c	The role of non-verbal behaviour as a means of communication and of facilitating and regulating verbal interaction.	
	C.11.2.d	Aspects of the way children think (such as ego-centrism) at different ages which affect their ability to communicate effectively.	
	C.11.2.e	The role of the adult in facilitating communication with a child.	
	C.11.2.f	The principles of active listening.	
	C.11.2.g	How to create and maintain a secure and safe environment for communicating with the child.	
	C.11.2.h	How to have child-led conversations.	
	C.11.2.i	The role of communication and self-expression in developing a child's self-esteem.	
	C.11.2.j	The importance of creating and maintaining a language-rich environment.	
	C.11.2.k	Understanding a child's right not to talk on occasions.	

USEFUL BOOKS

Babies and Young Children Book 1 – Development 0–7. Beaver *et al.* (1994) Stanley Thornes.
Head Start to Learning. J. Morrow (1988) Longman.
Practical Ways to Teach Reading. ed. C. Moon (1989) Ward Lock.
Play with a Purpose for the Under Sevens. E. Matterson (1989) Penguin.

PORTFOLIO ACTIVITY SUMMARY

Criteria	Portfolio page reference	0–1	1–4	4–7
C.11.2.a, b	See page 125 for Portfolio Activity			
C.11.2.c, d, i	See below for Portfolio Activity			
C.11.2.e	See below for Portfolio Activity			
C.11.2.g	See page 132 for Portfolio Activity			
C.11.2.j	See page 130 for Portfolio Activity			

C.11.2.a, C.11.2.b Portfolio Activity

See C.11.1.c on page 125.

C.11.2.c, C.11.2.d, C.11.2.i, C.17.4.a Portfolio Activity

You are in charge of a group of children aged 3–4 years. Think of an activity which will develop their self-esteem.

Consider:

    (a) Verbal and non-verbal communication;
    (b) Aspects of the way children think;
    (c) Cultural and environmental factors.

C.11.2.e, C.11.5.d Portfolio Activity

Tape record yourself talking with a young child (seven years or under).

Listen to the tape and assess your communication skills when talking with children.

How can you improve your own communication skills?

What practical steps could you take to assist the child's communication abilities?

C.11.2.f,   Describe a discussion session with young children which you have participated
C.11.2.h,   in/observed at your workplace/placement.
C.11.2.k

Consider these points.

(*a*) Was the session adult- or child-led?

....

(*b*) Did the session involve the children as active listeners?

....

(*c*) The child's right *not* to talk on occasions.

....

C.11.2.g Portfolio Activity

See C.11.3.c on page 132.

C.11.2.j Portfolio Activity

Design a nursery/classroom layout which will provide a language-rich environment. Support your plan of the layout with a short explanation of how it will support language.

C.11.3 Extend and reinforce children's communication skills

PROGRESS CHECKLIST	Criteria	Knowledge evidence	Date completed
	C.11.3.a	A variety of activities and games which give practice in and extend particular types of speech and communication; description, conversation, giving instructions and the rationale for using them.	
	C.11.3.b	A variety of activities and games which encourage the acting out of roles and give practice in the use of speech in various different contexts.	
	C.11.3.c	The role of positive feedback and encouragement in helping children to develop their communication skills.	
	C.11.3.d	The need to value the child's community language and the need to provide opportunities to develop it.	

USEFUL BOOKS

Bright Ideas for Early Years: Learning through Play. J. Morris and L. Mort (1991) Scholastic.
Bright Ideas: Word Games. M. Coles (1991) Scholastic.
Bright Ideas: Drama. J. Fulford, M. Hutching, A. Ross and H. Schmitz (1990) Scholastic.
Communicating with Children and Adults: Interpersonal skills for those working with babies and children. P. Petrie (1989) Edward Arnold.
Play with a Purpose for the Under Sevens. E. Matterson (1989) Penguin.
Bilingualism and the Bilingual. ed. S. Abudarham (1987) NFER Nelson (Chapter 9).

PORTFOLIO ACTIVITY SUMMARY

Criteria	Portfolio page reference	0–1	1–4	4–7
C.11.3.a, b	See page 132 for Portfolio Activity			
C.11.3.c	See page 132 for Portfolio Activity			
C.11.3.d	See page 132 for Portfolio Activity			

C.11.3.a, C.11.3.b Portfolio Activity

Devise a game to encourage children's listening and comprehension skills. Include details on: age group of children; purpose of game; possible learning outcomes for children/yourself; how the game was made.

C.11.3.c, C.11.1.a, C.11.2.g, C.11.4.c, C.11.5.a Portfolio Activity

Devise a reward system for use with young children. Outline how you would introduce the system to a specified age group of children and provide examples of the methods and materials used.

C.11.3.d, C.11.6.f Portfolio Activity

Find out what resources are available to children to encourage the development of their community language.

Compile a fact sheet using your findings, which will be useful to you in the future.

C.11.4 Promote children's communication skills in a group

<table>
<tr><td rowspan="7" style="writing-mode: vertical-rl">PROGRESS CHECKLIST</td><td>**Criteria**</td><td>**Knowledge evidence**</td><td>**Date completed**</td></tr>
<tr><td>C.11.4.a</td><td>How size of group and layout of environmental factors may affect communication.</td><td></td></tr>
<tr><td>C.11.4.b</td><td>A variety of activities and games and routines which give practice in and extend speech and communication such as description, conversation, giving instruction and role play and the rationale for using them.</td><td></td></tr>
<tr><td>C.11.4.c</td><td>The role of positive feedback and encouragement in helping children to develop their ability and confidence in communicating in group settings.</td><td></td></tr>
<tr><td>C.11.4.d</td><td>The stages and principles of children's social and emotional development in relation to group interactions.</td><td></td></tr>
<tr><td>C.11.4.e</td><td>The principles of how groups work and the adult's role in a group including the value of observing children's interaction before intervening.</td><td></td></tr>
<tr><td>C.11.4.f</td><td>The factors which may make children shy and withdrawn in group situations and how to encourage and assist those experiencing difficulty to communicate in a group.</td><td></td></tr>
</table>

USEFUL BOOKS

Bright Ideas for Early Years: Learning through Play. J. Morris and L. Mort (1991) Scholastic.
Bright Ideas: Word Games. M. Coles (1991) Scholastic.
Bright Ideas: Drama. J. Fulford, M. Hutching, A. Ross and H. Schmitz (1990) Scholastic.
Communicating with Children and Adults: Interpersonal skills for those working with babies and children. P. Petrie (1989) Edward Arnold.
Play with a Purpose for the Under Sevens. E. Matterson (1989) Penguin.
Bilingualism and the Bilingual. ed. S. Abudarham (1987) NFER Nelson (Chapter 9).
A Practical Guide to Child Observation. C. Hobart and J. Frankel (1994) Stanley Thornes.

From Birth to Five Years. M Sheridan (1987) NFER Nelson.
Understanding Your Child – A Parent's Guide to Child Psychology. R. Woolfson (1987) Faber and Faber (Development Checklists at end of book).
Babies and Young Children Book 1 – Development 0–7. Beaver *et al.* (1994) Stanley Thornes.

PORTFOLIO ACTIVITY SUMMARY

Criteria	Portfolio page reference	0–1	1–4	4–7
C.11.4.a	See page 125 for Portfolio Activity			
C.11.4.b	See below for Portfolio Activity			
C.11.4.c	See page 132 for Portfolio Activity			
C.11.4.f	See page 135 for Portfolio Activity			

C.11.4.a Portfolio Activity

See C.11.1.c on page 125.

C.11.4.b Portfolio Activity

Observe one child receiving and carrying out a three-part instruction from an adult. Comment on:

- *the child's ability to listen to the instruction;*
- *the child's ability to carry out the instruction;*
- *the child's understanding of the task;*
- *the emotional needs of the child;*
- *the degree of interaction with the adult;*
- *the language used by the child;*
- *the non-verbal communication displayed by the child.*

C.11.4.c Portfolio Activity

See C.11.3.c on page 132.

C.11.4.d   Find out about the stages and principles of children's social and emotional development in relation to communication skills. Then devise a checklist for the main stages of children's social and emotional development. How does the stage of development affect the child's ability to interact in a group?

C.11.4.e   **Role-Play Scenarios:**
Adult Intervention

Devise a role play to show when an adult should/should not intervene in children's play. Indicate whether the adult's intervention encourages or inhibits the children's language and communication.

....

Interpersonal Skills

Devise a role play for *one* of the following:

(*a*) meeting someone for the first time (e.g. a blind date);
(*b*) meeting with a colleague over a disagreement;
(*c*) staff meeting;
(*d*) parents' evening.

Consider these points.

(*i*)   Is the meeting formal/informal?
(*ii*) Which communication techniques are used?
(*iii*) What might be the possible outcome of the meeting?

....

If appropriate, act out your role plays with a group of fellow students/colleagues.

 ### C.11.4.f, C.11.5.e Portfolio Activity

Devise a game/activity which might encourage a shy and withdrawn child to participate within a group.

C.11.5 Help children to represent their experiences

PROGRESS CHECKLIST	Criteria	Knowledge evidence	Date completed
	C.11.5.a	A variety of practical activities, materials and techniques which encourage and help children to represent their experiences and the rationale behind them.	
	C.11.5.b	The value of drama/role play in representing a child's experience.	
	C.11.5.c	How children use many different situations and methods of representing/reflecting their life experience.	
	C.11.5.d	The role of the adult facilitator in helping a child to represent his/her experience and develop his/her ideas.	
	C.11.5.e	Common indicators of actual or potential difficulties that a child may communicate through representational activities.	
	C.11.5.f	The role of representation in developing and extending language and thought processes.	
	C.11.5.g	The sequence of development in children's drawing and painting and how to relate forms of representation to levels of development.	
	C.11.5.h	The importance of valuing the individual life and home experience of each child.	
	C.11.5.i	The interactive use of the four modes of language use i.e. listening, speaking, reading and writing.	

USEFUL BOOKS

The Excellence of Play. ed. J. Moynes (1994) Open University Press (Chapter 10).
Just Playing? J. Moynes (1993) Open University Press.
Bright Ideas in the Early Years: Learning Through Play. J. Morris and L. Mort (1991) Scholastic.
Creative Play. D. Einon (1986) Penguin; pp. 93–7.

PORTFOLIO ACTIVITY SUMMARY					
Criteria	Portfolio page reference	0–1	1–4	4–7
C.11.5.a	See page 132 for Portfolio Activity			
C.11.5.b	See below for Portfolio Activity			
C.11.5.c	See page 125 for Portfolio Activity			
C.11.5.d	See page 129 for Portfolio Activity			
C.11.5.e	See page 135 for Portfolio Activity			
C.11.5.g	See page 138 for Portfolio Activity			

 C.11.5.a Portfolio Activity

See C.11.3.c on page 132.

 C.11.5.b, C.11.6.g Portfolio Activity

Using a young child's own story or account of an event, work with them to create a book with pictures and captions.

Devise a role play about the child's story or event.

If possible, get the children at your workplace/placement to act out the role play.

Evaluate the successes and/or limitations of the role play.

 C.11.5.c Portfolio Activity

See C.11.1.c on page 125.

C.11.5.d Portfolio Activity

See C.11.2.e on page 129.

C.11.5.e Portfolio Activity

See C.11.4.f on page 135.

C.11.5.f,   Look at examples of children's drawings and paintings.
C.11.5.g
              Evaluate them in terms of age and stage of development.

              Check afterwards with the children's chronological age.

....

C.11.5.g, C.17.4.a Portfolio Activity

Observe a child's stage of development in drawing a human figure/a house. Include verbal questioning after completion e.g. 'Tell me about your picture.'

Evaluate the following elements.

> *(a) Progress – how the child performed the task e.g. comment on fine manipulative skills used, which part of figure was drawn first? Where on the paper did the child start?*
> *(b) Finished product – e.g. comment on patterns, cephlapods, significant detail, scale, proportion, number of digits, perspective, visual realism etc.*
> *(c) Response to questioning after completion of picture e.g. what did the child say when asked, 'Tell me about your picture', 'Which room is behind window?', 'Who lives in this house?'*
> *(d) Compare to expected stage of development.*

Include references and recommendations as appropriate. Also – personal learning – what did you learn by carrying out this observation?

Include child's drawing (a photocopy is acceptable).

C.11.5.h   See C.11.1.f on page 126.

C.11.5.i   Decode the following nursery rhyme:

> Ifz ejeemf ejeemf,
> Uif dbu boe uif gjeemf
> Uif dpx kvnqfe pwfs uid nppo;
> Uif mjuumf eph mbvhife,
> Up tff tvdi gvo,
> Boe uif ejti sbo bxbz xjui uif tqppo!

(Key: i = h)

Give an example of an activity for five- to six-year-olds which combines the four modes of language: listening, speaking, reading and writing.

....

C.11.6 Share books, stories and rhymes with children

	Criteria	Knowledge evidence	Date completed
PROGRESS CHECKLIST	C.11.6.a	The importance of the ways in which representation in books, stories and rhymes can reinforce or counteract stereotypes based on gender, racial origin, cultural and religious groups and disabilities.	
	C.11.6.b	The role of interest and participation in and enjoyment of spoken or written stories and rhymes in promoting children's language development.	
	C.11.6.c	Relevant criteria to evaluate books, stories and rhymes and examples to cover the range.	
	C.11.6.d	The importance of matching the book, story or rhyme with the development level of the child/children.	
	C.11.6.e	The key role played by books and stories and rhymes in language development and communication and in laying the foundations of early literacy.	
	C.11.6.f	The resources available in the community and how to use them including in the context of the promotion of a community second language.	
	C.11.6.g	How to make use of children's own stories and accounts of events.	
	C.11.6.h	How to use and/or make audio aids and visual aids.	
	C.11.6.i	How to adapt/design the presentation to enable the participation of children with sensory impairment.	

USEFUL BOOKS

The Education of the Young Child. ed. D. Fontana (1994) Basil Blackwell.
Becoming Literate. M. Clay (1992) Heinemann (Chapters 1 and 2).
Practical Ways to Teach Reading. C. Moon (1989) Ward Lock.
Children with Special Needs – A Guide for Parents and Carers. R. Woolfson (1991) Faber and Faber.

PORTFOLIO ACTIVITY SUMMARY				
Criteria	**Portfolio page reference**	**0–1**	**1–4**	**4–7**
C.11.6.b, c, d, e	See below for Portfolio Activity			
C.11.6.f	See page 132 for Portfolio Activity			
C.11.6.g	See page 137 for Portfolio Activity			
C.11.6.h	See page 141 for Portfolio Activity			
C.11.6.i	See page 141 for Portfolio Activity			

C.11.6.a   Give an example of a book you have used with young children that helped to counteract stereotypes. Outline how you used the book and give examples of the children's responses to the book.

....

C.11.6.b, C.11.6.c, C.11.6.d, C.11.6.e Portfolio Activity

Read a book to the children in your workplace/placement and carry out a follow-up activity linked to pre-reading/early reading and writing. Include information on how the children responded and provide examples of the children's work.

C.11.6.f Portfolio Activity

See C.11.3.d on page 132.

C.11.6.g Portfolio Activity

See C.11.5.b on page 137.

C.11.6.h Portfolio Activity

Design and make audio/visual aids to support children's learning. Choose two *of the following:*

      (a) language book;
      (b) musical instrument;
      (c) toy;
      (d) puppet.

Include details on: the age of the children; learning outcomes for the children/yourself; how the book/musical instrument/toy/puppet was made; implementation; evaluation; modifications; references/bibliography.

 ### *C.11.6.i Portfolio Activity*

Adapt/design a story to enable the participation of children with sensory impairment.

C.15 Contribute to the protection of children from abuse
Unit wide knowledge

	Criteria	Unit wide knowledge	Date completed
PROGRESS CHECKLIST	C.15.a	The overall course of children's development between 6 weeks and 8 years.	
	C.15.b	The needs and rights of young children and how these can be met.	
	C.15.c	Variations in parenting styles, family structures and relationships and how these may meet the needs of children in different ways.	
	C.15.d	The circumstances and pressures which make it more difficult for parents to meet the needs of children in different ways.	
	C.15.e	The rights and responsibilities of parents including their right to be informed and consulted throughout any procedures necessary for child protection.	
	C.15.f	The different forms that child abuse can take and the sorts of effects that abuse can have on children. This should indicate: physical abuse, neglect and failure to thrive, emotional abuse and sexual abuse.	
	C.15.g	The role of routine observations and record keeping in identification of possible abuse and for evidential purposes.	
	C.15.h	The legislative framework for child protection, key legal terms and the roles and responsibilities of key professionals including the social worker, health visitor, police officer, designated teacher and NSPCC Child Protection Officer (or NSPCC Inspector).	

USEFUL BOOKS

Babies and Young Children Book 2 – Work and Care. M. Beaver *et al.* (1995) Stanley Thornes.
Dictionary of Social Work. Martin Thomas and John Pieron. (1995)

 # Grid C.15

Please tick box when activity is complete.
P = *Portfolio Activity*

C.15.a	C.15.5.b	C.15.4.a	C.15.4.d	C.15.4.c	C.15.5.f	C.15.5.g	C.15.5.h	C.15.5.c	C.15.4.f	C.15.2.b
				P						

C.15.b	C.15.5.d	C.15.5.e
		P

C.15.c	C.15.1.c
	P

C.15.d	C.15.5.a

C.15.e	C.15.1.c	C.15.3.d	C.15.3.e	C.15.2.g	C.15.4.h
	P		P	P	P

C.15.f	C.15.1.a	C.15.2.f	C.15.2.c	C.15.2.a	C.15.1.h
		P			

C.15.g	C.15.1.e	C.15.1.d	C.15.1.b	C.15.4.g	C.15.3.a	C.15.3.b
						P

C.15.h	C.15.4.e	C.15.4.b	C.15.2.d	C.15.2.e	C.15.1.f	C.15.3.c	C.15.1.g	C.15.2.h
	P		P					

PORTFOLIO ACTIVITY SUMMARY		0–1	1–4	4–7
Criteria	**Portfolio page reference**			
C.15.a	See page 158 for Portfolio Activity			
C.15.b	See page 162 for Portfolio Activity			
C.15.c	See page 149 for Portfolio Activity			
C.15.e	See page 149 for Portfolio Activity			
C.15.f	See page 153 for Portfolio Activity			
C.15.g	See page 156 for Portfolio Activity			
C.15.h	See pages 153 and 159 for Portfolio Activities			

Contribute to the protection of children from abuse

C.15.a, C.15.b, C.15.c, C.15.d, C.15.e, C.15.f, C.15.g, C.15.h – See grid C.15 for cross-referenced knowledge evidence activities.

C.15.1 Identify signs and symptoms of possible abuse

	Criteria	Knowledge evidence	Date completed
PROGRESS CHECKLIST	C.15.1.a	The physical abuse, behaviour and emotional indicators which may signify possible abuse. These should include: Physical injuries, bruises and abrasions in unusual sites or configurations compared with those likely to have been inflicted by accident; inflammation, infection and bleeding of genital area and anus and other evidence of sexual activity; poor standards of hygiene, infection and infestation, weight loss or growth restriction and other physical signs of chronic neglect and failure to thrive. Self-destructive behaviours, unprovoked aggression and anti-social behaviour, withdrawal and isolation, inappropriate sexual play, precocious sexual/ sexualised behaviour, frozen watchfulness, eating disorders, sleep disturbance and nightmares, stress-linked enuresis, regression, over-compliance and indiscriminate affection and other symptoms of behavioural disturbance. Depression, mood swings, apathy, low self-esteem and other emotional indicators of possible abuse.	
	C.15.1.b	How to recognise, describe and record the appearance of bruises and other injuries and abrasions in different locations, and on different skin types (including use of diagrams as an aid and the importance of dating records).	
	C.15.1.c	A general awareness of the circumstances, lifestyles, relationships and any particular pressure on families whose children are in the care of the candidate.	
	C.15.1.d	Ways of observing and monitoring children for signs and symptoms of possible abuse.	
	C.15.1.e	The nature and uses of records of children's growth and the development and daily logs or accident and incident books.	

C.15.1.f	The child protection procedures of the setting/agency and how, when and to whom to report suspected abuse.	
C.15.1.g	The normal rules and boundaries of information sharing and confidentiality within the setting and the circumstances under which these may be breached.	
C.15.1.h	The influence of cultural, racial and gender stereotyping on interpretation of signs and symptoms of possible abuse, and how to counteract this.	

USEFUL BOOKS

Your assessor will have details of suitable reading material for this unit.

PORTFOLIO ACTIVITY SUMMARY

Criteria	Portfolio page reference	0–1	1–4	4–7
C.15.1.c	See page 149 for Portfolio Activity			

C.15.1.a   In order to understand child abuse it is extremely important that every individual has a clear definition of what constitutes 'abuse' and 'abusive behaviour'. Often we may assume that other people share our views and interpretations on child abuse. Also there can be some forms of behaviour which most people would consider to be abusive, but others would disagree. In order to help you think clearly and define your association to the differing forms of abuse complete the following:

What is abuse? (Take a wider view and make a comprehensive definition.)

....

What is child abuse?

....

Complete a definition in each of the following areas:

(*a*) physical abuse;

....

(*b*) neglect;

....

(*c*) emotional abuse;

....

(*d*) non-organic failure to thrive;

....

(*e*) sexual abuse;

....

(*f*) ritual/organised abuse.

....

Which of the following are signs of abuse and which are symptoms? Under the headings 'signs' and 'symptoms' draw up two separate lists.

Handslap marks

Aggression 'act up'

Dipping scalds

Grip marks

Bald patches

Self-mutilation

Show discomfort when walking

Poisoning (making a child drink bleach)

Burns or scalds in unusual positions or a definite shape

Restricted growth and development

Produce drawings of sex organs

Black eyes often caused by a direct blow

Sleep disturbance

Show extreme fear of a particular person

Stare blankly, unhappy, confused

Injuries to the genital or rectal area

Eating disorders

Low attainment or sudden changes in performance

Torn frenulum (the piece of skin inside the upper lip)

Act in a sexually inappropriate way towards adults

Bite marks often evident as bruising and teethmarks

X-rays that reveal past fractures or spinal fractures

Become hysterical when clothing is removed, particularly underclothes

C.15.1.b, C.15.1.d, C.15.1.e, C.15.3.a

List three types of detection methods that could be used and would be of particular value in a suspected child abuse case. Give reasons for your choice.

....

What is a percentile chart and what would it be used for?
Illustrate an example of a percentile chart.

....

In order to recognise and determine whether an injury to a child is accidental
or non-accidental it is important also to look at both the age of the child and
the development stage. On the following diagrams mark four different
locations and indicate the type of injury you feel would have been caused by
non-accidental injuries.

3-month-old baby   3-year-old child   6-year-old child

You have been presented with a suspected child abuse profile. Describe what
types of information you feel would be appropriate to the following categories,
giving examples:

(*a*) directly observed evidence;

....

(*b*) evidence from reliable sources;

....

(*c*) opinion and hearsay.

....

C.15.1.c, Describe how individual social pressures and limited family resources can
C.15.2.g, affect the development of a child.
C.15.3.e,
C.15.4.h

....

How can the care giver help both the child and a family to alleviate these
pressures and enhance the development of a child?

....

C.15.1.c, C.15.2.g, C.15.3.e, C.15.4.h *Portfolio Activity*

*Collect three articles on child abuse from newspapers or magazines. Look at the broader issue behind
the particular incidents. Detail your own account on some of these issues. See also tasks C.15.2.g,
C.15.3.e, C.15.4.h.*

C.15.1.f, How do you feel you could respond within your work setting to a child's
C.15.2.e   disclosure of abuse?

....

Discuss how your child protection procedures operate within your work
setting, including your response to confidentiality.

....

Why is it important to respect the principles of confidentiality?

....

C.15.1.g   Within the boundaries of sharing information and confidentiality, discuss how
you would feel about breaching confidentiality and under what circumstances
you would do this.

....

Discuss the following statement:
The role of the professional carer involves putting the needs of the child and
families before your own needs. It calls for a responsive attitude, the need to
be accountable and responsible, along with respecting all aspects of client
confidentiality.

....

C.15.1.h   Discuss the importance of cultural identity when interpreting signs and symptoms of suspected child abuse.

....

In order to counteract any form of stereotyping that could affect or influence your judgment about suspected child abuse list four factors to take into consideration when dealing with children from different cultural backgrounds.

....

C.15.2 Respond to a child's disclosure of abuse or neglect

	Criteria	Knowledge evidence	Date completed
P R O G R E S S C H E C K L I S T	C.15.2.a	The possible influence of cultural, racial, gender or other forms of stereotyping in response to a child who attempts to disclose abuse, and how to counteract this.	
	C.15.2.b	Ways of listening to and communicating with children of different ages including indicators of readiness to communicate and how to interpret both overt and covert messages.	
	C.15.2.c	The personal and emotional impact of child abuse, how to manage a controlled response to distressing disclosures and how to deal with the aftermath including appropriate sources of personal support.	
	C.15.2.d	The roles and responsibilities of relevant professionals to whom referral could be made or from whom advice/involvement could be sought with regard to possible disclosure and how and when to access their help.	
	C.15.2.e	The child protection procedures of the setting/agency and the candidate's own role and responsibilities within them.	
	C.15.2.f	The importance of reassurance and continued unconditional acceptance for the child in counteracting the potentially damaging effects of abuse and disclosure on self-image and self-esteem.	
	C.15.2.g	The potential impact of disclosure of abuse on other family members.	
	C.15.2.h	The legal requirements of evidence and the implications for a) involving an authorised professional at an early stage of disclosure; b) the importance of not pressurising the child, prompting or asking leading questions.	

152 NVQ/SVQ LEVEL 3 CHILD CARE AND EDUCATION

USEFUL BOOKS

Child Protection in Early Childhood Services. (Papers from a conference at the National Children's Bureau) Edited by G. Pugh, A. Hollows, (1994) National Children's Bureau ISBN 1 874579 19 9.

PORTFOLIO ACTIVITY SUMMARY		0–1	1–4	4–7
Criteria	Portfolio page reference			
C.15.2.d	See page 153 for Portfolio Activity			
C.15.2.f	See page 153 for Portfolio Activity			
C.15.2.g	See page 149 for Portfolio Activity			

C.15.2.a When involved with a disclosure from a child from a different cultural background, how could issues of both racial and gender stereotyping cloud your judgment?

....

What could you do to counteract these influences?

....

Discuss any difficulties you feel would be encountered when working with parents from different cultures, whose children's practice may differ from the norm.

....

C.15.2.b What do we mean by the term 'active listening'?

....

Pre-school children's disclosures of abuse are often difficult to hear and the child may be confused about what is happening. How then would you help a child to overcome this problem, in order to understand clearly what is or has been happening?

....

Give one example of the way in which you would interpret an 'overt' message from a child you suspect may be being sexually abused.

....

How would you interpret a 'covert' message if you suspect a child may be being abused (give one example)?

....

C.15.2.c,   Support for all carers involved with any form of child abuse situation is
C.15.4.g   important. Draw up a list of six points you feel would be necessary when
            working in the area of child protection.

....

From your list of six points, prioritise three main points you feel would be essential to the carer as a means of personal support.

....

How can the care worker ensure he/she has the necessary support within the workplace?

....

What do you feel would be the main stress factors you are likely to encounter when involved with a child abuse situation?

....

How do you feel you would control your own responses to stressful situations?

....

C.15.2.d Portfolio Activity

Research the roles of two professionals involved in child protection work. Write a detailed account of their roles and involvement along with any legal framework and including any limitations or restrictions.

Describe the procedures in relation to suspected child abuse in the following:

> *(a) a day care nursery;*
> *(b) reception class of an infant school.*

C.15.2.e   See C.15.1.f on page 149.

C.15.2.f Portfolio Activity

Scenario: *Baljeet is a four-year-old child whose behaviour is withdrawn and anxious following her disclosure of physical abuse. Anna, the key worker within the work setting, has been asked to draw up* *an action plan that will provide Baljeet with a supportive framework that is secure and will help Baljeet to develop self-image and self-esteem.*

Design and draw up the action plan Anna will use, taking into account cultural identity and practical ways in which to encourage Baljeet to see herself as an individual with value and worth. What activities can Baljeet be encouraged to join in with in order to promote acceptance of other children?

C.15.2.g   What are the short- and long-term consequences for 'the family' as a whole and for individual members, after a child's disclosure of abuse?

....

What help or support may be given to 'the family' and who would be involved?

....

C.15.2.g Portfolio Activity

See C.15.1.c on page 149.

C.15.2.h   What are the key principles of The Children's Act 1989?

....

What is the Area Child Protection Committee? Who could be involved with their work?

....

C.15.3 Provide information to other professions about child abuse

<table>
<tr><td>PROGRESS CHECKLIST</td><td>Criteria</td><td>Knowledge evidence</td><td>Date completed</td></tr>
<tr><td></td><td>C.15.3.a</td><td>How to evaluate and present different types of sources and the importance of distinguishing between directly observed evidence, evidence from reliable sources, opinion and hearsay.</td><td></td></tr>
<tr><td></td><td>C.15.3.b</td><td>How to appear confident and to be assertive when passing on information and expressing concerns to other professionals.</td><td></td></tr>
<tr><td></td><td>C.15.3.c</td><td>The professional groups most likely to want information and the purposes for which this information is likely to be required including the roles of case conferences and court proceedings.</td><td></td></tr>
<tr><td></td><td>C.15.3.d</td><td>The procedures of the setting with regard to rules and limits of confidentiality for supply of information to others and to security of any documents retained.</td><td></td></tr>
<tr><td></td><td>C.15.3.e</td><td>The rights of parents to access to information within the setting or passed to other professionals and when and how to share such information with them.</td><td></td></tr>
</table>

USEFUL BOOKS

Babies and Young Children Book 2 – Work and Care. Beaver *et al.* (1995) Stanley Thornes.

PORTFOLIO ACTIVITY SUMMARY

Criteria	Portfolio page reference	0–1	1–4	4–7
C.15.3.b	See page 156 for Portfolio Activity			
C.15.3.e	See page 149 for Portfolio Activity			

C.15.3.a   See C.15.1.b on page 147.

C.15.3.b Portfolio Activity

You are attending a case conference with other professionals about a child who attends your day care setting. The child is suspected of being physically abused, and you have expressed concerns over the issue raised by the Health Visitor, that the child 'appears to be unable to communicate'. You have been asked to discuss the issue.

Devise a fictional background for this scenario.

Using a tape recorder give the necessary background information on the child, followed by the child's behaviour within your work setting and any reference to concerns you may have here. Also make reference to the child's general development and any relationships with peers and staff. You need to look at the way you are confident that your information is correct, but also express any concerns you may have in an assertive manner to other professionals attending the case conference in order to bring about a valid conclusion.

C.15.3.c   You are attending a case conference at which it becomes apparent you will be asked to attend court proceedings. Describe the legal implications this may have for you, and how you would proceed with exchanging information with other professionals in line with issues of client confidentiality.

....

What type of information would be requested by an NSPCC Child Protection worker?

....

How would this information be used?

....

C.15.3.d,   What rights do parents have with regard to information you may hold about
C.15.3.e   suspected child abuse?

....

Assume you have been monitoring a child in your care for signs and symptoms of non-accidental injury.

(*a*) At what point do you feel it would be appropriate to pass this information on to other professionals?

....

(*b*) Would you allow the parents involved access to any of your information?

....

C.15.3.e Portfolio Activity

See C.15.1.c on page 149.

C.15.4 Care for a child who may have been abused

PROGRESS CHECKLIST	Criteria	Knowledge evidence	Date completed
	C.15.4.a	Ways in which children's development and behaviour may be affected by abuse.	
	C.15.4.b	Sources of expert help and advice for children whose behaviour gives cause for concern and how and when to access them.	
	C.15.4.c	The central role of self-esteem in moderating the effects of abuse; indicators of low self-esteem and how to promote self-esteem and the development of a positive self-image in children who may have been abused.	
	C.15.4.d	Methods of handling and managing difficult behaviour including the basic principles of behaviour modification.	
	C.15.4.e	Appropriate methods of communicating and negotiating with adults and children.	
	C.15.4.f	Ways of safely restraining children to prevent them hurting themselves or others.	
	C.15.4.g	How to control oneself and remain calm under stress.	
	C.15.4.h	The importance of the relationship with parents regardless of whether the relationship has been abusive and how to help children and parents build more positive relationships.	

USEFUL BOOKS

Babies and Young Children Book 1 – Development 0–7. (Chapter 12). Beaver *et al.* (1994) Stanley Thornes.

PORTFOLIO ACTIVITY SUMMARY

Criteria	Portfolio page reference	0–1	1–4	4–7
C.15.4.c	See below for Portfolio Activity			
C.15.4.e	See page 159 for Portfolio Activity			
C.15.4.h	See page 149 for Portfolio Activity			

C.15.4.a, The way in which the carer can give positive responses to a child's behaviour,
C.15.4.d, particularly in the case of child abuse, will help lessen the effects of abuse and
C.15.4.f   build on the child's self-image and self-esteem. Give four practical ways you
can manage challenging behaviour in a positive way.

....

Why would it be essential to keep any form of sanctions low key?

....

C.15.4.b   Describe how the following professionals could be involved with a child with a
behavioural concern, following abuse, and what their function and role would
be:

(*a*) child psychologist;

....

(*b*) play therapist.

....

C.15.4.c *Portfolio Activity*

When working with children who have been abused it is important to encourage self-expression, to enhance self-esteem and build on self-image. Draw up a list of 'put ups' you could use with children. Then draw up your list of 'put downs' that you would avoid using.

List two tasks that could be given to enable a child to develop self-esteem by building on success and achievement in the following age ranges:

(*a*) *2-year-old child;*

....

(*b*) *4-year-old child;*

....

(c) 6-year-old child.

....

C.15.4.d,   Consult Unit C.7 – 'Provide for the management of children's behaviour'.
C.15.4.f

C.15.4.e Portfolio Activity

Scenario: *You have observed Luke and Debbie playing in the home corner. Luke tells Debbie to lie on the floor and attempts to lie his body over Debbie, and bumps his body up and down. Debbie shouts, 'Get off me', pushing Luke away and begins to cry. Luke falls back on the carpet with a confused look on his face and starts to laugh. On further investigation with the children you suspect that Luke was attempting to 'act out' a sexually explicit act with Debbie. When you start to question Luke, he becomes very anxious and shouts, 'I didn't mean to hurt you, you should have been happy.' Luke then becomes very distressed and cries. Having discussed this incident with other staff you feel you have no grounds to suspect Luke is being abused, in fact one member of staff feels this behaviour is totally out of character for Luke. You therefore decide to invite Luke's parents in to discuss the situation.*

(a) *Discuss how you feel you are going to deal with this situation, including any action you would take with regard to Debbie's parents.*
(b) *Tape record any questions you feel you would be asking Luke's parents, remembering sensitivity.*
(c) *What skills do you feel would be needed in this situation?*

C.15.4.g   See C.15.2.c on page 153.

C.15.4.h   You are aware that a child in your care has been placed on the 'at risk' register. How could you help both child and parents to build a positive relationship?

....

C.15.4.h Portfolio Activity

See C.15.1.c on page 149.

C.15.5 Help children to protect themselves from abuse

	Criteria	Knowledge evidence	Date completed
PROGRESS CHECKLIST	C.15.5.a	The stresses of families and characteristics of children which make some children more vulnerable to abuse including overcrowding and impoverished environments, poor communication abilities, special needs, 'bonding' problems, e.g. arising from prematurity and other reasons for lack of responsiveness/rewardingness to parents etc.	
	C.15.5.b	Key stages in children's development and awareness of their body.	
	C.15.5.c	Opportunities provided within daily routines and different kinds of games and equipment that can help children become aware of their bodies.	
	C.15.5.d	The concept of children's rights and the importance of empowering children to exercise those rights.	
	C.15.5.e	The external factors and constraints that make it difficult for children's rights to be promoted.	
	C.15.5.f	Importance of building trust relationships within which children can talk about their concerns.	
	C.15.5.g	Activities and stories to encourage children to distinguish between affectionate touching and sexual touching, good and bad secrets.	
	C.15.5.h	Strategies for building children's self-confidence and assertiveness and ways of making the child care setting more responsive to children's concerns.	

USEFUL BOOKS

Keeping Safe – A Practical Guide to Talking to Children. Michelle Elliott (1988) New English Library.
Kidscape Under Fives Programme. Michelle Elliott (1993) Hodder & Stoughton.

PORTFOLIO ACTIVITY SUMMARY				
Criteria	**Portfolio page reference**	**0–1**	**1–4**	**4–7**
C.15.5.e	See page 162 for Portfolio Activity			

C.15.5.a   Social research has indicated that various characteristics of families and individuals within society make some children more vulnerable to abuse. Discuss this statement providing evidence to support your argument.

....

Why are children with special needs and specific disabilities particularly vulnerable to all forms of abuse?

....

Give two environmental causes relating to child abuse.

....

C.15.5.b,   What are the key stages in the development of a child that can make him/her open to child abuse?

....

C.15.5.c   How can you encourage children through themes and topics to be assertive and gain the confidence which will contribute to their own self-protection?

....

Devise a 'what if' list for use with children in your work setting. State the age of the children it would be used with.

....

C.15.5.d,   Given that all children have the right to basic needs, give four examples of
C.15.5.e   rights you feel all children should have.

....

What is the purpose of the Children's Legal Centre?

....

What is the function of United Convention on the Rights of The Child and when was it formed?

....

C.15.5.e Portfolio Activity

Design and illustrate the following posters with the use of statistics from magazine articles, surveys, charitable organisations etc.

(a) *A poster that promotes and supports children's rights in the UK.*
(b) *A poster that promotes International Child's Rights.*

C.15.5.f   What qualities must the carer demonstrate in order to form a trusting relationship with a child who has been abused?

....

Why is it important for the carer to refer to a professionally authorised person in the early stages of a child's disclosure of abuse?

....

How would you ensure that you do not put a child who is involved in disclosure under any unnecessary pressure?

....

Investigation of suspected child abuse is referred from which two main sources?

....

Define what is referred to in the following terms:

(a) partial disclosure;
(b) full disclosure.

....

C.15.5.g   Locate two books for use with children that would help a child understand Stranger Danger. State the age of the children you would use the books with and your reasons for your choice. Set out your answers as follows:

Title   ....

Author: ....

ISBN: ....

Reason for choice: ....

List two activities you could use with children (stating the age of the children) that would help them to understand:

(*a*) bullying;
(*b*) ways in which children can be assertive and protect themselves;
(*c*) safe secrets and unsafe secrets.

....

C.15.5.h   Record two examples of how the carer within the work setting can encourage children to have 'rights'.

....

Give three strategies you would operate in your work setting that develop children's assertiveness and self-confidence.

....

C.16 OBSERVE AND ASSESS THE DEVELOPMENT AND BEHAVIOUR OF CHILDREN
UNIT WIDE KNOWLEDGE

	Criteria	Unit wide knowledge	Date completed
PROGRESS CHECKLIST	C.16.a	Detailed knowledge of the course of children's physical development, sensory and intellectual development, social and emotional development and language and communication skills between 6 weeks and 8 years.	
	C.16.b	The range of behaviours which might be expected of children at different ages and stages of development.	
	C.16.c	The principles underlying different types of observation and assessment methods and possible sources of bias in their use.	
	C.16.d	The policy and rules of the organisation and setting in regard to observation, assessment and record keeping and confidentiality in records.	
	C.16.e	The roles of other professionals in regard to observations and assessments with particular reference to co-operation in assessment, sharing of information and confidentiality issues.	
	C.16.f	The need for parental involvement and approval in observation and assessment and the contributions that parents can make from their extensive knowledge of their own child.	
	C.16.g	The rights of children when being observed and assessed and the continuing responsibilities of adults for others in the child care setting.	

USEFUL BOOKS

A Practical Guide to Child Observation. C. Hobart and J. Frankel (1994) Stanley Thornes.
From Birth to Five Years. M. Sheridan (1987) NFER Nelson.
Babies and Young Children Book 1 – Development 0–7. Beaver *et al.* (1994) Stanley Thornes.
Profiling, Recording and Observing – A Resource Pack for the Early Years. B. Steiner *et al.* (1993) Routledge.

 # *Grid C.16*

Please tick box when activity is complete.
P = *Portfolio Activity*

C.16.a	C.16.3.c	C.16.3.b	C.16.3.e
			P

C.16.b		C.16.1.c	C.16.2.e
		P	

C.16.c	C.16.1.d	C.16.1.e	C.16.1.f	C.16.1.g	C.16.1.h	C.16.1.a
			P	P	P	
	C.16.1.b	C.16.2.h	C.16.2.b	C.16.2.c	C.16.2.d	C.16.2.f
	P	P	P		P	P

C.16.e	C.16.2.i	C.16.2.j	C.16.2.g	C.16.3.f
			P	P

C.16.f		C.16.3.g
		P

C.16.g	C.16.2.a	C.16.3.a	C.16.3.d
	P	P	

PORTFOLIO ACTIVITY SUMMARY		0–1	1–4	4–7
Criteria	Portfolio page reference			
C.16.a	See page 174 for Portfolio Activity			
C.16.b	See page 168 for Portfolio Activity			
C.16.c	See pages 168, 169, 171 and 172 for Portfolio Activities			
C.16.d	See below for Portfolio Activity			
C.16.e	See pages 172 and 174 for Portfolio Activities			
C.16.f	See page 174 for Portfolio Activity			
C.16.g	See page 174 for Portfolio Activity			

C.16 Observe and assess the development and behaviour of children

C.16.a, C.16.b, C.16.c – See grid C.16 for cross-referenced knowledge evidence activities.

 ### C.16.d Portfolio Activity

Find out the policy and rules of the organisation, setting or your workplace in regard to observation, assessment and record keeping and confidentiality of records.

C.16.e, C.16.f, C.16.g – See grid C.16 for cross-referenced knowledge evidence activities.

C.16.1 Carry out observations of a child's behaviour

	Criteria	Knowledge evidence	Date completed
PROGRESS CHECKLIST	C.16.1.a	The rationale for observing children's spontaneous or naturally occurring behaviour in comparison to that which is contrived for the purposes of assessment.	
	C.16.1.b	Cultural, social and gender based influences on children's spontaneous or naturally occurring behaviour.	
	C.16.1.c	How and why young children's behaviour may vary across situations, with time of day and other factors.	
	C.16.1.d	The reasons why it is important to observe a child's behaviour on a number of occasions and in different situations.	
	C.16.1.e	How to and why record the features of the context when making observations of children's spontaneous or naturally occurring behaviour.	
	C.16.1.f	The uses of technology in carrying out and recording observations of children's spontaneous or naturally occurring behaviour.	
	C.16.1.g	How to select and use appropriate methods for observing and recording different aspects of children's spontaneous or naturally occurring behaviour.	
	C.16.1.h	The role of the non-interventionist observer.	

USEFUL BOOKS

A Practical Guide to Child Observation. C. Hobart and J. Frankel (1994) Stanley Thornes.
From Birth to Five Years. M. Sheridan (1987) NFER Nelson.
Babies and Young Children Book 1 – Development 0–7. Beaver *et al.* (1994) Stanley Thornes.
Profiling, Recording and Observing – A Resource Pack for the Early Years. B. Steiner *et al.* (1993) Routledge.

Criteria	Portfolio page reference	0–1	1–4	4–7
PORTFOLIO ACTIVITY SUMMARY				
C.16.1.b	See below for Portfolio Activity			
C.16.1.c	See below for Portfolio Activity			
C.16.1.f	See page 169 for Portfolio Activity			
C.16.1.g	See page 169 for Portfolio Activity			
C.16.1.h	See page 169 for Portfolio Activity			

C.16.1.a   Why do you think it is important to observe children's spontaneous or naturally occurring behaviour in comparison to that which is contrived for the purposes of assessment? Record your thoughts.

....

C.16.1.b, C.16.2.h Portfolio Activity

Carry out observations in your workplace/setting of children's spontaneous play. Evaluate them looking at cultural, social and gender based influences which may have affected their behaviour.

C.16.1.c Portfolio Activity

Design a simple task to be completed by the child. Carry out an observation three times during the day and compare the similarities and differences in the performance of the child. Suggest why you think they have occurred.

C.16.1.d   List three different ways in which you have observed young children, including formal and informal methods of observation, different situations and observations over a period of time.

....

What is the importance of these methods of observation?

....

C.16.1.e   When making observations of children's naturally occurring behaviour it is important to include the context in which this behaviour has occurred. Suggest two ways of recording features of the context, and give reasons for your choices.

....

C.16.1.f Portfolio Activity

See C.16.2.g on page 172.

C.16.1.g Portfolio Activity

When recording different aspects of children's behaviour it is important to select and use appropriate methods of recording. Carry out five observations using different methods of observing and recording. Evaluate your observations looking at physical, intellectual, social and emotional development. Suggest which method of recording would be most appropriate for giving information to parents/carers, child's new teacher, health visitor, educational psychologist and speech therapist.

C.16.1.h Portfolio Activity

To gain a true picture of a child's development it is important to use a variety of observational techniques. The non-interventionist observer can play an important role in developing care/curriculum plans. Carry out an observation in the role of the non-interventionist. In your evaluation describe the role of the non-interventionist observer and discuss what you found difficult/easy about this style of observation.

C.16.2 Observe a child's performance at specific tasks and activities

<table>
<tr><th></th><th>Criteria</th><th>Knowledge evidence</th><th>Date completed</th></tr>
<tr><td rowspan="9" style="writing-mode: vertical-lr">PROGRESS CHECKLIST</td><td>C.16.2.a</td><td>The rationale for observing a child's performance at specific tasks and activities and ways in which information obtained can be used.</td><td></td></tr>
<tr><td>C.16.2.b</td><td>How to select tasks and activities and appropriate recording formats to meet the agreed goals and purposes of observation.</td><td></td></tr>
<tr><td>C.16.2.c</td><td>Possible sources of distractions/disruptions during observation of task performance and how to minimise these.</td><td></td></tr>
<tr><td>C.16.2.d</td><td>How to communicate instructions or requests effectively to children of different ages and characteristics in a one-to-one situation.</td><td></td></tr>
<tr><td>C.16.2.e</td><td>How and why young children's behaviour may vary across test situations and the reasons why repeated observations are sometimes necessary including links between concentration, performance and distractibility.</td><td></td></tr>
<tr><td>C.16.2.f</td><td>How to and why record features of the context and off task behaviours when making observations of children's performance and distractibility.</td><td></td></tr>
<tr><td>C.16.2.g</td><td>The uses of technology in presenting tasks or stimuli and recording children's performance on specific tasks and activities.</td><td></td></tr>
<tr><td>C.16.2.h</td><td>Possible cultural, social and gender based influences on children's responses to structured test/assessment situations.</td><td></td></tr>
<tr><td>C.16.2.i</td><td>The various roles that an observer/facilitator might play in enabling a child to demonstrate his/her full potential.</td><td></td></tr>
</table>

C.16.2.j	The importance of standardisation of tasks, context and the role of the observer/facilitator in some formal test situations.	

USEFUL BOOKS

A Practical Guide to Child Observation. C. Hobart and J. Frankel (1994) Stanley Thornes.
From Birth to Five Years. M. Sheridan (1987) NFER Nelson.
Babies and Young Children Book 1 – Development 0–7. Beaver *et al.* (1994) Stanley Thornes.
Profiling, Recording and Observing – A Resource Pack for the Early Years. B. Steiner *et al.* (1993) Routledge.

PORTFOLIO ACTIVITY SUMMARY

Criteria	Portfolio page reference	0–1	1–4	4–7
C.16.2.a	See page 174 for Portfolio Activity			
C.16.2.b	See below for Portfolio Activity			
C.16.2.d	See page 172 for Portfolio Activity			
C.16.2.g	See page 172 for Portfolio Activity			
C.16.2.h	See page 168 for Portfolio Activity			

C.16.2.a Portfolio Activity

See C.16.3.a on page 174.

C.16.2.b Portfolio Activity

Select a task for a child to complete which demonstrates fine manipulative skills. Design two appropriate recording formats which will meet the agreed goals and purposes of the observation. Carry out the observation using your task and recording formats. In your evaluation discuss how appropriate your task and recording formats were.

C.16.2.c   Suggest how to minimise possible sources of distractions/disruptions during observation of task performance.

C.16.2.d Portfolio Activity

When giving instructions or communicating requests to children it is of the utmost importance to communicate effectively. Report on how you communicate requests/instructions to children of different ages. How could you adapt or improve your communication skills?

C.16.2.e,   Why is it important to observe a child doing the same task on a number of
C.16.2.f   different occasions?

....

Why should you record the context of off task behaviours?

....

C.16.2.g, C.16.1.f Portfolio Activity

Present a task to a child using technology, for example sound lotto or a computer game.

Record the child's performance using an audio cassette or video camera. After the child has completed the task continue to record the activity that they choose to go to next. Provide an evaluation in which you should discuss how you would use this method of observation in assessment purposes.

C.16.2.h Portfolio Activity

See C.16.1.b on page 168.

C.16.2.i   As an observer/facilitator you will carry out a variety of roles in order to enable children to demonstrate their full potential. Describe some of the techniques you have used or may use.

....

C.16.2.j   Why is it important to standardise tasks, the context and the role of the observer/facilitator in some formal test situations?

....

Suggest one formal test that is carried out under these conditions.

....

C.16.3 Utilise the results of observations

	Criteria	Knowledge evidence	Date completed
PROGRESS CHECKLIST	C.16.3.a	What counts as significant evidence from observations and the concepts of validity and reliability and factors which affect this.	
	C.16.3.b	How to interpret and summarise data from observations and assessments.	
	C.16.3.c	How to relate examples of observed and assessed behaviour to 'widely accepted norms of behaviour'.	
	C.16.3.d	How to use observations for the purposes of assessment and the limitations of such uses.	
	C.16.3.e	How to use assessments of development/abilities/behaviour to help develop care plans or curriculum plans or individualised learning programmes.	
	C.16.3.f	How to present information keyed to goals in an effective and appropriate way.	
	C.16.3.g	The importance of liaising with parents and other professionals when assessing children's behaviour, abilities and development.	

USEFUL BOOKS

A Practical Guide to Child Observation. C. Hobart and J. Frankel (1994) Stanley Thornes.
From Birth to Five Years. M. Sheridan (1987) NFER Nelson.
Babies and Young Children Book 1 – Development 0–7. Beaver *et al.* (1994) Stanley Thornes.

PORTFOLIO ACTIVITY SUMMARY

Criteria	Portfolio page reference	0–1	1–4	4–7
C.16.3.a, f	See below for Portfolio Activity			
C.16.3.e	See below for Portfolio Activity			
C.16.3.g	See below for Portfolio Activity			

 ### *C.16.3.a, C.16.3.f, C.16.2.a Portfolio Activity*

Investigate reasons for using checklists. What significance would this type of assessment play alongside observation in developing curriculum plans?

C.16.3.b,   After carrying out observations and assessments you will need to interpret,
C.16.3.c   summarise and evaluate the data you have collected and relate it to 'widely accepted norms of behaviour' in an objective way. Find out which are the most widely used.

....

C.16.3.d   Describe how you have used observations for the purposes of assessment. What are the limitations of this?

....

 ### *C.16.3.e Portfolio Activity*

Observe a child in the workplace/setting over a period of five minutes. Evaluate your observation looking at the child's physical, intellectual, emotional and social development. Use your observation to develop a care or curriculum plan or individualised learning programme.

 ### *C.16.3.g Portfolio Activity*

Carry out an observation of one area of a child's development e.g. pre-reading skills. Liaise with parent(s) to use their extensive knowledge of their own child's abilities and liaise with other professionals in your workplace/setting to use their knowledge of the child's abilities. Complete the observation yourself, adding to the information evidence you have collected by direct observation. Colour code the data you collect so you can see what information has been given by parents, colleagues and collected by your own observations.

C.14 CARE FOR AND PROMOTE THE DEVELOPMENT OF BABIES
UNIT WIDE KNOWLEDGE

	Criteria	Unit wide knowledge	Date completed
PROGRESS CHECKLIST	C.14.a	A knowledge of the growth and development of babies up to 12 months and how this can be affected by the social, emotional and physical environment.	
	C.14.b	Standards of hygiene and safety which should be maintained when working with babies.	
	C.14.c	How caring for babies may vary with different cultures and individual needs.	

USEFUL BOOKS

From Birth to Five Years. M. Sheridan (1987) NFER Nelson.
Caring for the under 8s. Jennie and Lance Lindon (1993) Macmillan.
Babies and Young Children Book 1 – Development 0–7. Beaver *et al.* (1994) Stanley Thornes.

✔ *Grid C.14*

Please tick box when activity is complete.

P = *Portfolio Activity*

C.14.a	C.14.1.a	C.14.1.b	C.14.1.c	C.14.1.d	C.14.1.e	C.14.1.h	C.14.2.b
	P	P	P	P		P	P
	C.14.2.c	C.14.2.d	C.14.2.g	C.14.3.a	C.14.3.b	C.14.3.c	C.14.3.d
	P				P	P	P
	C.14.3.e	C.14.4.a	C.14.4.b	C.14.4.c	C.14.4.d	C.14.4.e	C.14.5.a
	P			P			P
	C.14.5.b	C.14.5.c	C.14.5.d	C.14.5.e			
	P	P	P	P			

C.14.b	C.14.2.a	C.14.2.e
	P	P

C.14.c	C.14.1.f	C.14.1.g	C.14.2.f
	P		P

PORTFOLIO ACTIVITY SUMMARY				
Criteria	Portfolio page reference	0–1	1–4	4–7
C.14.a	See pages 178, 180, 181, 182, 184, 188, 189, 191 and 193 for Portfolio Activities			
C.14.b	See pages 184 for Portfolio Activities			
C.14.c	See pages 181 and 185 for Portfolio Activities			

Care for and promote the development of babies

 ### C.14.a Portfolio Activity

'Development involves four aspects, physical, intellectual, emotional and social and each is dependent on each other.'

Extract from Caring for Young Children, *P. Geraghty (1994) Bailliere Tindall.*

Design a booklet entitled 'Growth and Development 0–12 months'. Include as much information as possible, for example:

    (a) *detailed description of the newborn;*

    (b) *descriptions of the assessments made to check health and development of the newborn;*

    (c) *explanation of how the physical, social and emotional environment affects development of babies 0–12 months.*

C.14.b   See grid C.14 for cross-referenced knowledge evidence activities.

C.14.c   Give a detailed description of how three cultures (you may choose which) care for their babies.

....

Discuss how babies' individual needs may vary when caring for babies of the following ages:

(a) 0–4 weeks;

....

(b) 1–3 months;

....

(c) 4–6 months;

....

(d) 6–12 months.

....

C.14.1 Fulfil the nutritional needs of babies

PROGRESS CHECKLIST	Criteria	Knowledge evidence	Date completed
	C.14.1.a	Alternative types of milk for use with breast-fed babies and methods of storing expressed milk.	
	C.14.1.b	The general nutritional requirements of babies at different ages and what constitutes a balanced diet.	
	C.14.1.c	Methods of food and drink preparation and preservation, and hygiene and safety requirements associated with these.	
	C.14.1.d	The process of weaning and factors which influence it.	
	C.14.1.e	The wider function of feeding as a sensory experience and how early experiences of feeding can shape attitudes to food.	
	C.14.1.f	The common dietary requirements including those associated with religious and cultural practices.	
	C.14.1.g	The common food allergies and feeding difficulties and where to get advice about them.	
	C.14.1.h	Advantages and disadvantages of breast and bottle feeding.	

USEFUL BOOKS

Child Development. G. Hutchinson and S. Oliver (1989) Blackie.
Caring for Children. P. Geraghty (1994) Bailliere Tindall.

PORTFOLIO ACTIVITY SUMMARY

Criteria	Portfolio page reference	0–1	1–4	4–7
C.14.1.a	See below for Portfolio Activity			
C.14.1.b	See below for Portfolio Activity			
C.14.1.c	See page 181 for Portfolio Activity			
C.14.1.d	See page 181 for Portfolio Activity			
C.14.1.f	See page 181 for Portfolio Activity			
C.14.1.h	See page 182 for Portfolio Activity			

C.14.1.a Portfolio Activity

Research the topic 'infant feeding'. You may gather information from a paediatric unit at your local hospital and from parents. Compare, discuss and evaluate your findings and write up a detailed report which should include:

> *(a) alternative types of milk for use with breast-fed babies;*
> *(b) methods of storing expressed milk.*

What are the practices in your placement?

C.14.1.b Portfolio Activity

Design a booklet containing detailed information on the general nutritional requirements of babies.

> *(a) Give the nutritional requirements of a child aged:*
> *0–4 weeks;*
> *1–3 months;*
> *4–6 months;*
> *6–12 months.*

> *(b) Give the constituents of a balanced diet for a child aged:*
> *0–4 weeks;*
> *1–3 months;*
> *4–6 months;*
> *6–12 months.*

A section of the booklet should include a table to show the nutrients in 200 ml of breast, cows' and modified milk when made up.

Devise a main meal and a snack for a one-year-old child which promotes healthy eating.

C.14.1.c Portfolio Activity

Plan an activity to show different methods of food preparation to feed a six-month-old child. Record results and write a conclusion. Include preferences and give reasons.

Write out a set of instructions explaining how to present and preserve food and drink for babies.

Hygiene and safety requirements are important in infant feeding. Observe a child during meal times. What are the aspects of hygiene and safety? Record and evaluate.

C.14.1.d Portfolio Activity

Plan a chart to show stages of weaning in a child aged:

4 months;
4½ months;
5 months;
6–7 months;
8–12 months.

Prepare an information booklet about weaning. Include:

> *(a) types of food;*
> *(b) flavour consistency;*
> *(c) feeding skills;*
> *(d) do's and dont's.*

C.14.1.e   Think about your experiences of eating as a very young child. Discuss 'the effects of early experiences of feeding'. Your discussion should include:

(*a*) feeding as a sensory experience;
(*b*) attitudes towards food;
(*c*) the role of food in shaping behaviour and attitudes;
(*d*) a conclusion.

....

C.14.1.f Portfolio Activity

Collect information on diets from parents from different cultures. Draw up a chart giving information about different religious and cultural practices.

Plan a menu for a child:

> *(a) with a medical condition;*
> *(b) from a named culture;*
> *(c) from a named religion.*

Discuss how the dietary needs of children from different cultures and religious practices are met at your workplace/placement.

C.14.1.g Discuss with parents the dietary requirements and feeding difficulties of their children. You may collect information from other sources.

What are the common food allergies?

....

What diets are required to deal with them?

....

Where can advice be given for them?

....

Describe two common feeding difficulties.

....

Choose one and explain how you would deal with it.

....

Where can the parents get advice on feeding difficulties?

....

 ### *C.14.1.h Portfolio Activity*

Why is breast-feeding usually considered the best option for a baby? Design a booklet on this topic. The following should be included:

    (a) reasons for breast feeding;
    (b) how to encourage this;
    (c) the advantages;
    (d) possible difficulties;
    (e) the ways in which these difficulties may be solved.

Why is it essential to bottle feed some babies? Design a leaflet explaining this to a parent. The following should be included:

    (a) reasons for bottle feeding;
    (b) keeping the equipment sterilised;
    (c) the advantages of bottle feeding;
    (d) the disadvantages.

C.14.2 Manage the physical care of babies

	Criteria	Knowledge evidence	Date completed
PROGRESS CHECKLIST	C.14.2.a	The general health and hygiene requirements of babies at different stages.	
	C.14.2.b	Recognise when a baby needs sleep/rest and how to provide for it.	
	C.14.2.c	The variation in sleep patterns in babies over time and across individuals.	
	C.14.2.d	The importance of rest/sleep or quiet periods as part of the daily routine and of matching the routines of the home and child care setting.	
	C.14.2.e	The emotional issues around toilet training and knowing when and how to introduce it.	
	C.14.2.f	Unusual conditions and symptoms of common ailments which may require to be reported.	
	C.14.2.g	Awareness of changes in temperature and the need to adapt the environment and clothing accordingly.	

USEFUL BOOKS

Caring for Children. P. Geraghty (1994) Bailliere Tindall.

PORTFOLIO ACTIVITY SUMMARY		0–1	1–4	4–7
Criteria	Portfolio page reference			
C.14.2.a	See below for Portfolio Activity			
C.14.2.b, d	See below for Portfolio Activity			
C.14.2.c	See below for Portfolio Activity			
C.14.2.e	See below for Portfolio Activity			
C.14.2.f	See page 185 for Portfolio Activity			

C.14.2.a Portfolio Activity

Design a booklet giving detailed information about health and hygiene for a child aged 0–12 months. Include a questionnaire.

C.14.2.b, C.14.2.d Portfolio Activity

Record the patterns of sleep/rest of four babies over a period of time. Prepare a booklet for parents.

What factors should be considered for sleep/rest for a baby? Explain how to provide for sleep/rest for a baby in the sleeping environment.

C.14.2.c Portfolio Activity

Observe children at rest/sleep over a period of time. Ages:

> *1 year;*
> *4 years;*
> *7 years.*

Discuss variations in sleep/rest patterns.

C.14.2.e Portfolio Activity

Discuss with parents/colleagues issues surrounding potty training. Review a book on this topic, then evaluate. Information should include:

> *(a) how and when to potty train;*
> *(b) effects of potty training on emotions of child and adults.*

C.14.2.f   Sick children need special care. Collect as much information as you can on this subject.

Which unusual conditions require reporting? Give reasons.

....

Which six symptoms of common ailments may require to be reported? Give reasons.

....

Which conditions can be sensibly treated by parents? Give reasons.

....

Recommendations: Include difference in care of a sick one-year-old and a sick six-year-old.

....

What are placement procedures for:

(*a*) administration of drugs/treatment?

....

(*b*) dealing with sick children?

....

How would you treat an unconscious baby?

....

C.14.2.f Portfolio Activity

Devise booklet entitled 'Caring for Sick Children' using unit wide knowledge.

C.14.2.g   Why is it important to be aware of changes in a baby's temperature when working with babies?

High temperature: effects and treatments.

....

Low temperature: effects and treatments.

....

Adapting the clothing to the temperature.

....

How can a carer ensure that the child's temperature is maintained?

....

How can the environment be adapted to the temperature?

....

C.14.3 Promote the physical growth and development of babies

	Criteria	Knowledge evidence	Date completed
PROGRESS CHECKLIST	C.14.3.a	The needs and requirements of babies at different ages with respect to physical growth and development and how these needs might be met.	
	C.14.3.b	The general role of exercise and physical play in promoting physical growth and development and how exercise and physical play can be incorporated into physical routines.	
	C.14.3.c	Suitable safety equipment for use with babies of different sizes and ages up to 12 months.	
	C.14.3.d	Types of equipment and activities which can be used to promote babies' physical development.	
	C.14.3.e	How to provide a suitable environment to promote stimulation.	

USEFUL BOOKS

Babies and Young Children Book 1 – Development 0–7. Beaver *et al.* (1994) Stanley Thornes.
Babies and Young Children Book 2 – Work and Care. Beaver *et al.* (1995) Stanley Thornes.

PORTFOLIO ACTIVITY SUMMARY

Criteria	Portfolio page reference	0–1	1–4	4–7
C.14.3.b	See page 188 for Portfolio Activity			•
C.14.3.c, d	See page 189 for Portfolio Activity			
C.14.3.e	See page 189 for Portfolio Activity			

C.14.3.a   'In the 1950s a psychologist called Abraham Maslow proposed a theory which is still widely accepted. It suggests that human behaviour and development depend on certain needs being met.'

Extract from *Human Development*, M. Miller *et al.* (1992) Churchill Livingstone.

What are the needs of babies? How does meeting these needs affect growth and development?

0–4 weeks

....

3–6 months

....

6–9 months

....

9–12 months

....

How can an adult meet these needs? Include examples and case histories (if possible).

0–4 weeks

....

3–6 months

....

6–9 months

....

9–12 months

....

 ## C.14.3.b Portfolio Activity

How can exercise and physical play promote the physical growth and development of babies?

Plan some activities which can be incorporated into physical routines. Implement. Record in detail and evaluate.

What modifications would you make? Why?

C.14.3.c, C.14.3.d Portfolio Activity

Draw up a chart to show activities/equipment suitable for babies. The following should be included:

    (a) *age of child;*
    (b) *development stage;*
    (c) *types of equipment and activities;*
    (d) *suitability and safety of equipment;*
    (e) *effects on physical growth and development.*

Research and write up a detailed essay entitled: 'Choosing Safety Equipment for Babies'.

C.14.3.e Portfolio Activity

Design a poster for a parent explaining how to provide a suitable environment to stimulate a baby.

What should be considered in a bedroom in order to create a stimulating environment for a child?

C.14.4 Provide stimulation to foster the development of babies

<table>
<tr><td rowspan="5" style="background:black;color:white">PROGRESS CHECKLIST</td><td>**Criteria**</td><td>**Knowledge evidence**</td><td>**Date completed**</td></tr>
<tr><td>C.14.4.a</td><td>The importance of stimulation and interaction with adults to the development of babies up to 12 months.</td><td></td></tr>
<tr><td>C.14.4.b</td><td>Toys and equipment suitable for babies up to 12 months.</td><td></td></tr>
<tr><td>C.14.4.c</td><td>The links between physical play and experiences and intellectual development.</td><td></td></tr>
<tr><td>C.14.4.d</td><td>Provision of a suitable environment to provide stimulation.</td><td></td></tr>
</table>

USEFUL BOOKS

Caring for the under 8s. Jennie and Lance Lindon (1993) Macmillan.

PORTFOLIO ACTIVITY SUMMARY

Criteria	Portfolio page reference	0–1	1–4	4–7
C.14.4.c	See page 191 for Portfolio Activity			

C.14.4.a   Why is it important to stimulate babies?

....

Discuss the ways in which an adult can interact with babies to promote development.

....

C.14.4.b   Describe a range of toys and equipment suitable for babies up to 12 months.

....

C.14.4.c Portfolio Activity

Set up an activity that would demonstrate the links between physical play and experiences and the development of intelligence in babies. Implement. Discuss results with colleagues. Evaluate and record. Make some recommendations.

C.14.4.d   Babies need stimulation. How can you provide a suitable environment to provide the stimulation they need?

....

C.14.5 Promote the language of babies

<table>
<tr><td rowspan="6" style="text-align:center">PROGRESS CHECKLIST</td><td>**Criteria**</td><td>**Knowledge evidence**</td><td>**Date completed**</td></tr>
<tr><td>C.14.5.a</td><td>The sequence and development of language and communication skills in babies and factors which influence learning and development.</td><td></td></tr>
<tr><td>C.14.5.b</td><td>Suitable books and stories for babies to support the development of language.</td><td></td></tr>
<tr><td>C.14.5.c</td><td>Games, rhymes and songs suitable for babies up to 12 months.</td><td></td></tr>
<tr><td>C.14.5.d</td><td>The importance of turn taking and conversational language.</td><td></td></tr>
<tr><td>C.14.5.e</td><td>Methods of encouraging attentive listening and sound discrimination in babies of different ages.</td><td></td></tr>
</table>

USEFUL BOOKS

Babies and Young Children Book 1 – Development 0–7. Beaver *et al.* (1994) Stanley Thornes.
Caring for the under 8s. Jennie and Lance Lindon (1993) Macmillan.

PORTFOLIO ACTIVITY SUMMARY

Criteria	Portfolio page reference	0–1	1–4	4–7
C.14.5.a	See page 193 for Portfolio Activity			
C.14.5.b	See page 193 for Portfolio Activity			
C.14.5.c	See page 193 for Portfolio Activity			
C.14.5.d, e	See page 193 for Portfolio Activity			

C.14.5.a Portfolio Activity

Design a booklet explaining communication and language development. Sections should include:

     (a) information and discussions explaining patterns of how language develops;
     (b) a chart to show the stages in children's language development up to 12 months;
     (c) factors (no less than 7) affecting language development. Give examples in each case.

C.14.5.b Portfolio Activity

Review a book suitable for a 12-month-old. Write a brief report which could be read by parents considering buying it. Reports should cover, for example, drawings, paintings, text and colour.

What other books would you recommend?

C.14.5.c Portfolio Activity

Make up four games for babies of ages 0–4 weeks, 3–6 months, 6–9 months and 9–12 months. Try them out with children or discuss with colleagues. Evaluate the design of the games and whether they could be improved.

Review a book of rhymes and songs for babies up to 12 months. Prepare a criteria for selecting suitable books. Discuss. Make recommendations if necessary.

C.14.5.d, C.14.5.e Portfolio Activity

Observe four children of different ages up to 12 months. Assess their levels of communication/language development. Plan relevant experiences and activities to meet each child's individual needs. Record in detail.

Include:

     (a) circumstances of observations and techniques;
     (b) description and explanation of plans made to promote language development;
     (c) strategies used for interaction with child/adult;
     (d) encouraging feedback – why, how?

M.4 WORK WITH COLLEAGUES IN A TEAM

UNIT WIDE KNOWLEDGE

	Criteria	Unit wide knowledge	Date completed
PROGRESS CHECKLIST	M.4.a	A general basic knowledge of group dynamics.	
	M.4.b	The structure, role and policies of the organisation.	
	M.4.c	The roles and areas of responsibility of self and other team members.	
	M.4.d	Equal opportunities codes of practice of the organisation.	
	M.4.e	The basic principles of accountability and responsibility.	

USEFUL BOOKS

People in Organisations. Edward Sallis and Kate Sallis (Chapters 15, 19 and 20). (1990) Macmillan.
Special Issues in Child Care. M. O'Hagan and M. Smith (1994) Bailliere Tindall.

✓ Grid M.4

Please tick box when activity is complete.
P = *Portfolio Activity*

M.4.a

M.4.4.d	M.4.4.e	M.4.4.f	M.4.4.g
	P	P	P
M.4.5.a	M.4.5.b	M.4.5.d	M.4.5.e
		P	P

M.4.b

M.4.1.c	M.4.1.e	M.4.1.g	M.4.1.h	M.4.3.a
P	P	P	P	P

M.4.c

M.4.1.b	M.4.1.d	M.4.1.f	M.4.3.f	M.4.3.g
P	P	P	P	
M.4.3.h	M.4.3.i	M.4.3.j	M.4.4.a	
P	P	P	P	

M.4.d

M.4.4.b	M.4.4.c	M.4.4.h	M.4.5.c
P	P		

M.4.e

M.4.1.a	M.4.2.a	M.4.2.b	M.4.2.c	M.4.2.d	M.4.2.e
P				P	P
M.4.2.f	M.4.2.g	M.4.3.b	M.4.3.c	M.4.3.d	M.4.3.e
P	P	P	P		P

PORTFOLIO ACTIVITY SUMMARY

Criteria	Portfolio page reference	0–1	1–4	4–7
M.4.a	See pages 198 and 205 for Portfolio Activities			
M.4.b	See pages 198 and 202 for Portfolio Activities			
M.4.c	See pages 198 and 205 for Portfolio Activities			
M.4.d	See page 202 for Portfolio Activity			
M.4.e	See pages 198, 200, 202 and 203 for Portfolio Activities			

M.4 Work with colleagues in a team

M.4.a, M.4.b, M.4.c, M.4.d, M.4.e – See grid M.4 for cross-referenced knowledge based activities.

M.4.1 Contribute to the work of the team

PROGRESS CHECKLIST	Criteria	Knowledge evidence	Date completed
	M.4.1.a	Procedures of meetings and the process of decision making.	
	M.4.1.b	The importance of collective responsibility.	
	M.4.1.c	The organisational structure and the roles within it including team members.	
	M.4.1.d	The importance of collective responsibility.	
	M.4.1.e	Aims and objectives of the team.	
	M.4.1.f	Awareness of personal needs and the needs of others in the team.	
	M.4.1.g	The team's role in relation to others within and external to the organisation.	
	M.4.1.h	The necessity for confidentiality.	

USEFUL BOOKS

People in Organisations. Edward Sallis and Kate Sallis (Chapters 15, 19 and 20). (1990) Macmillan.
Special Issues in Child Care. M. O'Hagan and M. Smith (1994) Bailliere Tindall.

PORTFOLIO ACTIVITY SUMMARY

Criteria	Portfolio page reference	0–1	1–4	4–7
M.4.1.a, b, d–h	See page 198 for Portfolio Activity			
M.4.1.c	See page 198 for Portfolio Activity			

M.4.1.a, M.4.1.b, M.4.1.d, M.4.1.e, M.4.1.f, M.4.1.g, M.4.1.h, M.4.2.d, M.4.2.g, M.4.3.e, M.4.3.f, M.4.3.h, M.4.3.i, M.4.3.j, M.4.4.g Portfolio Activity

After reading Chapter 15 in People in Organisations *by Edward and Kate Sallis, and Chapter 10 in* Special Issues in Child Care *by Maureen O'Hagan and Maureen Smith, decide whether you are able to:*

    (a) attend a meeting within your workplace/setting;
    (b) attend a meeting at your local playgroup, school or church organisation;
    (c) tape an appropriate meeting from a selected television programme.

Prepare an evaluation report upon your chosen method of observing a meeting using the following criteria.

    (a) Have they used the procedures and format laid down in the text from the above stated books?
    (b) How do you think they arrived at the chosen topic for discussion?
    (c) What preparation and planning do you feel may have gone into the meeting beforehand?
    (d) What were the aims and objectives of the meeting?
    (e) Who took responsibility for certain areas?
    (f) Do you feel that the group took on an amount of responsibility – how were tasks delegated?
    (g) What would you say were the strengths and weaknesses of the team individually?
    (h) Did anyone ask for minutes or reports to be compiled?
    (i) Was confidentiality breached at any stage?
    (j) What methods of communication were used throughout the procedure and how effective were they?
    (k) Did the group show commitment as a whole – was this addressed correctly?

Lastly, if it were possible that you could have been part of that particular team meeting, state how you would perceive your role, the responsibility that you would have, and your areas of strength and weakness.

 M.4.1.c Portfolio Activity

Read Chapter 13 of People in Organisations *by Edward and Kate Sallis. Draw a diagram to explain the structure of the organisation in your workplace/setting.*

M.4.2 Contribute to team meetings

	Criteria	Knowledge evidence	Date completed
PROGRESS CHECKLIST	M.4.2.a	The importance of collective responsibility.	
	M.4.2.b	The significance of commitment and what affects it.	
	M.4.2.c	Effective communication in a team meeting – both verbal and non-verbal.	
	M.4.2.d	The procedures for group meetings and the presentation of reports.	
	M.4.2.e	The need to appraise and evaluate the effects of meetings and of procedures.	
	M.4.2.f	What and how to prepare in advance.	
	M.4.2.g	Expectations and norms for behaviour in given meetings.	

USEFUL BOOKS

Your assessor should have details of suitable reading material for this unit.

PORTFOLIO ACTIVITY SUMMARY

Criteria	Portfolio page reference	0–1	1–4	4–7
M.4.2.d	See page 198 for Portfolio Activity			
M.4.2.e, f, g	See page 200 for Portfolio Activity			

M.4.2.a   State why it is important to have responsibility as a group.

....

M.4.2.b   Explain the significance of commitment and what may affect it.

....

M.4.2.c   Describe methods of communication within a team meeting – both verbal and non-verbal. Indicate which would be in your opinion the more effective.

....

M.4.2.d Portfolio Activity

See M.4.1.a on page 198.

M.4.2.e, M.4.2.f, M.4.2.g Portfolio Activity

Where possible, observe a meeting within your workplace. Prepare a report upon your observation of:

    (a) what and how items were prepared in advance;
    (b) the effectiveness of the meeting and the procedure it followed;
    (c) the behaviour expected and observed throughout.

M.4.2.g Portfolio Activity

See also M.4.1.a on page 198.

M.4.3 Contribute to the development of good practice of the team

Criteria	Knowledge evidence	Date completed
M.4.3.a	Current practice and objectives of the organisation.	
M.4.3.b	The information sharing systems of the organisation.	
M.4.3.c	The value of development of the team through training, consultation and the support of individuals and how this is effected.	
M.4.3.d	When to bring in or suggest the use of outside resources.	
M.4.3.e	The value and potential of own contribution to team development.	
M.4.3.f	How to share ideas with other members of the team.	
M.4.3.g	How to give and receive directions and instructions.	
M.4.3.h	Awareness of own role in team decision making.	
M.4.3.i	Awareness of own personal responsibility to follow through ideas and how to do it.	
M.4.3.j	Awareness of own role in the evaluation of team development.	

PROGRESS CHECKLIST

USEFUL BOOKS

Your assessor will have details of suitable reading material for this unit.

PORTFOLIO ACTIVITY SUMMARY		0–1	1–4	4–7
Criteria	**Portfolio page reference**	**0–1**	**1–4**	**4–7**
M.4.3.a	See below for Portfolio Activity			
M.4.3.b	See below for Portfolio Activity			
M.4.3.c	See below for Portfolio Activity			
M.4.3.e, f, h, i, j	See page 198 for Portfolio Activity			
M.4.3.g	See page 203 for Portfolio Activity			

M.4.3.a Portfolio Activity

Using a prospectus placement you have worked in, choose four of their objectives and state how the current practice reflects them.

Also state how a supervisor could ensure that good practice was encouraged and bad practice eliminated.

M.4.3.b Portfolio Activity

Research within your workplace how staff are made aware of new information and how targets are planned and monitored.

Can you make any suggestions towards making this more effective?

M.4.3.c, M.4.4.b, M.4.4.c Portfolio Activity

Produce an information booklet/cardex system for yourself. This should contain information on support services available to you and colleagues at a future date. It should include agencies involved in:

      (a) training and education;
      (b) counselling;
      (c) equal opportunities;
      (d) health and safety.

M.4.3.d   When would it be appropriate to bring in outside resources?

....

M.4.3.e, M.4.3.f, M.4.3.h, M.4.3.i, M.4.3.j Portfolio Activity

See M.4.1.a on page 198.

 ### *M.4.3.g Portfolio Activity*

State a task (that you have recently learned to do) i.e. an activity with the children.
Describe how you acquired the knowledge to do this activity – was this difficult or easy? Include the communication you had with staff prior to implementation.
Include a report of how you carried out the activity with the children step by step, and evaluate the activity in the terms of learning outcomes for the children and yourself.

M.4.4 *Contribute to support for colleagues*

	Criteria	Knowledge evidence	Date completed
PROGRESS CHECKLIST	M.4.4.a	Support systems within the organisation.	
	M.4.4.b	Sources of information about support in the wider community.	
	M.4.4.c	Sources of information about support in the wider community.	
	M.4.4.d	The value of praise and positive feedback.	
	M.4.4.e	The nature and limits of working relationships according to the setting.	
	M.4.4.f	The nature and characteristics of professionalism in this field.	
	M.4.4.g	The different levels of communication operating within the team and the organisation.	
	M.4.4.h	Potential areas of stress, conflict and discrimination.	

USEFUL BOOKS

Your assessor will have details of suitable reading material for this unit.

PORTFOLIO ACTIVITY SUMMARY

Criteria	Portfolio page reference	0–1	1–4	4–7
M.4.4.a	See page 205 for Portfolio Activity			
M.4.4.b, c	See page 202 for Portfolio Activity			
M.4.4.e, f	See page 205 for Portfolio Activity			
M.4.4.g	See page 198 for Portfolio Activity			

M.4.4.a Portfolio Activity

Describe the support systems within your organisation.

State who you could go to for help and support with:

> (a) *three situations that caused the most distress;*
> (b) *four skills that you need to acquire;*
> (c) *two problems with the organisation.*

M.4.4.b, M.4.4.c Portfolio Activity

See M.4.3.c on page 202.

M.4.4.d   Look back at the task for M.4.3.g. Think about how praise and positive reinforcement affected the outcomes.

   (*a*) What praise and reinforcement did you give?

   ....

   (*b*) What other methods could you use in the future?

   ....

M.4.4.e, M.4.4.f, M.4.5.d, M.4.5.e Portfolio Activity

Scenario: *During a morning at work you go to fetch something from a cupboard in the corridor. As you shut the door of the cupboard you see a colleague coming out of the staff room. As she/he doesn't speak you assume that she/he did not see you.*

You reflect that it is an odd time for someone to be in the staff room. You later discover that a purse has gone missing from the staff room.

Name four alternatives for dealing with this situation.
What would be the consequences of each method?
Which method would you therefore choose?

M.4.4.g Portfolio Activity

See M.4.1.a on page 198.

M.4.4.h   State where there may be potential areas of stress, conflict and discrimination within the workplace/setting.

   ....

M.4.5 Respond to conflict within the team

<table>
<tr><th rowspan="12" style="writing-mode: vertical-rl">PROGRESS CHECKLIST</th><th>Criteria</th><th>Knowledge evidence</th><th>Date completed</th></tr>
<tr><td>M.4.5.a</td><td>Understand that conflicts are a natural part of working life.</td><td></td></tr>
<tr><td>M.4.5.b</td><td>How, when and where to discuss and seek resolution of conflict.</td><td></td></tr>
<tr><td>M.4.5.c</td><td>Understanding of grievance procedures.</td><td></td></tr>
<tr><td>M.4.5.d</td><td>The importance of not allowing conflict to affect the work of the organisation.</td><td></td></tr>
<tr><td>M.4.5.e</td><td>Areas of potential conflict and a range of strategies to deal with the situation.</td><td></td></tr>
</table>

USEFUL BOOKS

Your assessor will have details of suitable reading material for this unit.

PORTFOLIO ACTIVITY SUMMARY

Criteria	Portfolio page reference	0–1	1–4	4–7
M.4.5.c	See page 207 for Portfolio Activity			
M.4.5.d, e	See page 205 for Portfolio Activity			

In task M.4.4.a you looked at the types of conflicts that arise in a working situation, and who would be there to support you. It is vitally important when working with children that any conflict does not spill over into your work with them. Read Chapter 19 in *People in Organisations* and look carefully at the sections relating to how groups behave and develop.

M.4.5.a   Describe a conflict that you have had in the workplace or within another area familiar to you (remember the rule of confidentiality).

....

What did you do to resolve the conflict?

....

In hindsight do you think this was the best way to resolve it and why?

....

Can you think of any other way it could have been resolved?

....

How did/could this conflict have affected your work, and what did/should you have done to prevent this?

....

M.4.5.b,   Name ten ways that people can be discriminated against in the workplace
M.4.5.d   (e.g. race).

....

What would you do about any two of these issues?

....

(If you find out about organisations remember to put their details in your information system – M.4.3.c.)

M.4.5.c Portfolio Activity

Research the correct grievance procedure that should be in place within the workplace/setting, that can be put into motion if and when a certain conflict cannot be resolved.

M.4.5.d and M.4.5.e Portfolio Activity

See M.4.4.e on page 205.

M.7 Plan, implement and evaluate activities and experiences to promote children's learning and development unit wide knowledge

	Criteria	Unit wide knowledge	Date completed
PROGRESS CHECKLIST	M.7.a	Detailed knowledge of the course of children's physical development, social and emotional development, sensory and intellectual development and language and communication skills between 6 weeks and 8 years.	
	M.7.b	How to observe children.	
	M.7.c	The processes of planning and evaluation.	
	M.7.d	How to analyse and assess information.	
	M.7.e	The boundaries of confidentiality for the setting and how and when and to whom information can be passed.	

Useful books

Assessment in Early Childhood Education. Geva M. Blenkin and A.V. Kelly (1992) Paul Chapman Publishing.
A Practical Guide to Child Observation. Christine Hobart and J. Frankel (1994) Stanley Thornes.

Grid M.7

Please tick box when activity is complete.
P = *Portfolio Activity*

M.7.a	M.7.2.1
	P

M.7.b	M.7.3.c
	P

	M.7.3.a	M.7.3.b	M.7.2.a	M.7.2.h	M.7.1.1	M.7.3.d	M.7.3.e
M.7.c	P	P	P	P	P	P	P
	M.7.3.f	M.7.3.g	M.7.3.h	M.7.1.g	M.7.1.h	M.7.1.i	M.7.1.d
	P	P	P		P	P	P

	M.7.1.a	M.7.1.j	M.7.2.i	M.7.1.b	M.7.1.c	M.7.2.j	M.7.2.k
M.7.d		P	P	P	P		
	M.7.2.b	M.7.2.c	M.7.1.e	M.7.1.f	M.7.2.d	M.7.2.g	M.7.2.f
	P	P	P		P		

	M.7.2.m	M.7.1.k	M.7.2.e
M.7.e	P		P

PORTFOLIO ACTIVITY SUMMARY

Criteria	Portfolio page reference	0–1	1–4	4–7
M.7.a	See page 216 for Portfolio Activity			
M.7.b	See page 218 for Portfolio Activity			
M.7.c	See pages 212, 215 and 218 for Portfolio Activities			
M.7.d	See pages 212, 213, 215 and 216 for Portfolio Activities			
M.7.e	See below and page 216 for Portfolio Activities			

M.7 Plan, implement and evaluate activities and experiences to promote children's learning and development

M.7.a, M.7.b, M.7.c, M.7.d – See grid M.7 for cross-referenced knowledge based activities.

M.7.e Portfolio Activity

You have a new member of staff within your workplace setting. Draw up guidelines relating to the boundaries of confidentiality for the setting and state how and when and to whom information can be passed.

M.7.1 Plan activities and experiences to facilitate children's learning and development

	Criteria	Knowledge evidence	Date completed
PROGRESS CHECKLIST	M.7.1.a	The need for planning to be based on observation and assessment of individual children.	
	M.7.1.b	The background and previous experience of the children in the group.	
	M.7.1.c	The need for a balance in activities and experiences to ensure breadth of experience and learning, progression, continuity and the opportunity to practise skills.	
	M.7.1.d	The need to plan activities which reflect the social and cultural background of the children and which promote equal opportunities.	
	M.7.1.e	The relevance and value of particular individual and group activities in promoting children's learning and development.	
	M.7.1.f	How to match activities to needs and level of development for the individual child or group.	
	M.7.1.g	When and how to involve children in planning.	
	M.7.1.h	How to plan within a given time frame.	
	M.7.1.i	The need to take account of health and safety issues when planning.	
	M.7.1.j	The need to take account of health and safety issues when planning.	
	M.7.1.k	The resources available in the community.	
	M.7.1.l	The role that other workers (including class teachers if appropriate to the setting) play in providing an overall framework for curriculum planning.	

USEFUL BOOKS

Assessment in Early Childhood Education. Geva M. Blenkin and A.V. Kelly (1992) Paul Chapman Publishing.
A Practical Guide to Child Observation. Christine Hobart and J. Frankel (1994) Stanley Thornes.

PORTFOLIO ACTIVITY SUMMARY

Criteria	Portfolio page reference	0–1	1–4	4–7
M.7.1.b, d, h, i, l	See below for Portfolio Activity			
M.7.1.c, e, j	See page 213 for Portfolio Activity			

M.7.1.a   State reasons why you think it is important to plan upon observations and assessments made.

....

From your experience within the workplace and from your observations, how would you communicate to a child's parents/parental carer about their specific needs? What suggestions/support would you offer for the following:

(*a*) A child who requires a lot of encouragement and one-to-one work, plus often demonstrates aggressive behaviour within a group situation.

....

(*b*) A child who displays a good knowledge of the overall activities and concepts available to them. He/she often asks for extra activities to complete.

....

M.7.1.b, M̄.7.1.d, M.7.1.h, M.7.1.i, M.7.1.l Portfolio Activity

Choose a theme that could be carried out for a term within the workplace.

Make a note of points to be considered when implementing your chosen theme under the following headings:

> (a) *the National Curriculum;*
> (b) *health and safety issues;*
> (c) *social and cultural backgrounds of the children.*

From your ideas, decide upon some activities that you could implement within the first week of the new theme and plan a timetable showing these.

M.7.1.c, M.7.1.e, M.7.1.j Portfolio Activity

During your normal planning for the week's activities, your colleagues and yourself have observed that a percentage of the children have become easily distracted, and a percentage of the children have easily achieved success.

> (a) *What does this suggest?*
> (b) *Plan for the week taking into account the needs of the children and pinpointing a specific time when you would incorporate extending activities and how you would achieve this.*

M.7.1.f,   Think of times and occasions during the day at your workplace when children
M.7.1.g   could be encouraged to take part in the planning of an activity.

State the appropriate times and occasions.

....

When planning the activity with a group of children how would you ensure that each child had ample opportunity to contribute and participate during both the discussion and the activity?

....

How much input would you have?

....

How would you carry it out effectively?

....

M.7.1.k,   List the resources and other professionals that you would anticipate are
M.7.2.e   available to aid and enhance your provision of activities within the local
            community of your workplace.

....

Describe how you could implement the resources and other professionals.

....

M.7.2 Implement activities and experiences planned for children

	Criteria	Knowledge evidence	Date completed
PROGRESS CHECKLIST	M.7.2.a	The need for implementation broadly to reflect planning intentions.	
	M.7.2.b	How to provide appropriate activities in an attractive, imaginative and stimulating way.	
	M.7.2.c	How and when to provide activities which are calming and soothing.	
	M.7.2.d	How to use your time and the children's time effectively.	
	M.7.2.e	Where and how to obtain and use material and human resources.	
	M.7.2.f	How to use and adapt existing and readily available resources in an innovative and flexible manner.	
	M.7.2.g	How to use space effectively, imaginatively and safely.	
	M.7.2.h	How to make the best use of indoor and outdoor environments in implementing plans.	
	M.7.2.i	The need to adapt or modify planned activities to suit children's needs and interests and to capitalise on unplanned learning opportunities.	
	M.7.2.j	The characteristics and potential uses of a variety of equipment and material suitable for young children.	
	M.7.2.k	The health and safety requirements of the setting.	
	M.7.2.l	Periods of time for which children at various stages of development are capable of sustaining concentration.	
	M.7.2.m	Simple record keeping techniques.	

USEFUL BOOKS

Your assessor will have details of suitable reading material for this unit.

PORTFOLIO ACTIVITY SUMMARY				
Criteria	**Portfolio page reference**	**0–1**	**1–4**	**4–7**
M.7.2.a, h	See below for Portfolio Activity			
M.7.2.b, j, k	See below for Portfolio Activity			
M.7.2.c, d, e, i	See page 216 for Portfolio Activity			
M.7.2.l	See page 216 for Portfolio Activity			
M.7.2.m	See page 216 for Portfolio Activity			

M.7.2.a, M.7.2.h Portfolio Activity

Study the inside and outside area/environment of your workplace.

> *(a) Draw up a plan of both and include a description of the areas, stating the provision provided.*
> *(b) Name themes/topics that you could implement and carry out within these environments, making sure that you consider the National Curriculum.*
> *(c) Plan on themes/topics thoroughly in the form of a spidergram, incorporating both environments.*

M.7.2.b, M.7.2.j, M.7.2.k Portfolio Activity

You have been asked to set up and establish a new playgroup/nursery setting, or you are contemplating becoming a registered child minder.

Collate information on the wide variety of equipment and materials available for such a setting.

Using the information, draw up a chart showing the skills gained from the items chosen.

Research the health and safety requirements that you would have to implement within the new setting, and include your findings.

Also plan the setting, showing the areas within such a setting that you would include, and how you would present the environment in an attractive and inviting way.

M.7.2.c, M.7.2.d, M.7.2.e, M.7.2.i Portfolio Activity

Plan a timetable showing a variety of activities, and indicate where you would implement the calmer, quieter ones, taking into account the needs and interests of the children, plus the time available to carry out the activities.

M.7.2.e   See M.7.1.k on page 213.

M.7.2.f,   How could you adapt the home corner or a disused area within the workplace
M.7.2.g   to encourage imaginative play?

....

Describe how you would adapt a corner of the setting when you only have a large cardboard box, two coloured drapes and a variety of paint and paper available to you.

....

How could you implement or extend this area into other activities within your workplace, or the outside environment?

....

M.7.2.1 Portfolio Activity

Within your appropriate workplace, and throughout your course, make observations upon a child's concentration within the stated age range, with a particular activity to suit the age of the child, and compare them.

State reasons for your choice of activity and how you could extend it (if necessary) to encourage the child's concentration span.

Age range 1–4 years and 4–7 years.

M.7.2.m Portfolio Activity

State the principles for record keeping within the workplace.

Devise a record keeping system to be used within the workplace upon the children on a:

- *daily;*
- *weekly;*
- *termly;*
- *yearly basis.*

M.7.3 *Evaluate activities and experience planned for children*

<table>
<tr><td rowspan="10" style="text-align:center">PROGRESS CHECKLIST</td></tr>
<tr><td>Criteria</td><td>Knowledge evidence</td><td>Date completed</td></tr>
<tr><td>M.7.3.a</td><td>The purpose of evaluation.</td><td></td></tr>
<tr><td>M.7.3.b</td><td>How to set and use criteria for evaluation.</td><td></td></tr>
<tr><td>M.7.3.c</td><td>Methods of monitoring, observing and recording for evaluation purposes.</td><td></td></tr>
<tr><td>M.7.3.d</td><td>Methods of self-evaluation.</td><td></td></tr>
<tr><td>M.7.3.e</td><td>How to present evaluation information in suitable forms for different people/purposes.</td><td></td></tr>
<tr><td>M.7.3.f</td><td>How to use evaluation information in further planning.</td><td></td></tr>
<tr><td>M.7.3.g</td><td>How to link evaluation to children's development.</td><td></td></tr>
<tr><td>M.7.3.h</td><td>How to contribute to team evaluation as appropriate.</td><td></td></tr>
</table>

USEFUL BOOKS

Your assessor will have details of suitable reading material for this unit.

PORTFOLIO ACTIVITY SUMMARY

Criteria	Portfolio page reference	0–1	1–4	4–7
M.7.3.a, b	See page 218 for Portfolio Activity			
M.7.3.c, h	See page 218 for Portfolio Activity			
M.7.3.d, e	See page 218 for Portfolio Activity			
M.7.3.f, g	See page 218 for Portfolio Activity			

M.7.3.a, M.7.3.b Portfolio Activity

Give reasons why evaluation is an important aspect within a setting.

Draw up an evaluation sheet, showing appropriate headings for a particular child.

With the permission of your workplace and the parents'/parental carers', use your evaluation sheet upon the child.

Comment upon your findings.

M.7.3.c, M.7.3.h Portfolio Activity

State those methods of monitoring, observing and recording known to you.

With this information plan out a proposed role play for a staff meeting about staff development.

Within your proposed role play, state the strengths within the team and areas which need strengthening.

Include an action plan for each member of staff.

M.7.3.d, M.7.3.e Portfolio Activity

Evaluate yourself in front of a mirror and from this plan a worksheet to show this information.

Research and gather other methods of self-evaluation and state ways in which you could use these with children, plus how you could display this.

Plan an evaluation sheet that would be suitable for use within the workplace and for parents to observe upon request.

M.7.3.f, M.7.3.g Portfolio Activity

Collate pieces of children's work. These must be either drawings/paintings or forms of written work.

From your observations of the work, decide if they show on average the right age and stage of development for the individual child.

State ways in which the pieces of work may be useful in planning further activities and whether the particular child has been set work at the correct level.

Plan an individual programme for one of the children to help develop him/her with a particular area of his/her work.

M.8 PLAN, IMPLEMENT AND EVALUATE ROUTINES FOR YOUNG CHILDREN

UNIT WIDE KNOWLEDGE

	Criteria	Unit wide knowledge	Date completed
PROGRESS CHECKLIST	M.8.a	The overall course of children's development between 6 weeks and 8 years.	
	M.8.b	How routines affect children's development.	
	M.8.c	Strategies for observing individual children and children in groups.	
	M.8.d	Methods of gathering information for implications for children's routines.	
	M.8.e	How to analyse and assess information for implications for children's routines.	
	M.8.f	Relevant personnel in other agencies, their different roles and how to assess their expertise.	
	M.8.g	The process of planning and evaluation.	
	M.8.h	The process of planning and evaluation.	
	M.8.i	Effects of seasonal variations and weather on the nature of activities and contingency arrangements.	
	M.8.j	The boundaries of confidentiality for the setting and how, when and to whom information can be passed.	

USEFUL BOOKS

Babies and Young Children Book 1 – Development 0–7. Beaver *et al.* (1994) Stanley Thornes.

✓ # *Grid M.8*
Please tick box when activity is complete.
P = *Portfolio Activity*

M.8.a	M.8.1.a	M.8.2.b	M.8.3.g
	P	P	P

M.8.b	M.8.2.a	M.8.2.d

M.8.c	M.8.1.b	M.8.1.c	M.8.2.f
		P	P

M.8.d	M.8.1.f	M.8.2.k	M.8.2.l	M.8.3.c
	P	P	P	P

M.8.e	M.8.2.h	M.8.3.a	M.8.3.b	M.8.3.h
	P	P	P	P

M.8.f	M.8.1.j	M.8.1.d
	P	P

M.8.g	M.8.2.c	M.8.2.e

M.8.h	M.8.1.g	M.8.1.h	M.8.1.i	M.8.2.g	M.8.2.j	M.8.3.d	M.8.3.f
	P	P	P	P			P

M.8.i	M.8.1.e	M.8.2.i
		P

M.8.j	M.8.3.e

Criteria	Portfolio page reference	0–1	1–4	4–7
PORTFOLIO ACTIVITY SUMMARY				
M.8.a	See pages 223 and 230 for Portfolio Activities			
M.8.c	See pages 223 and 227 for Portfolio Activities			
M.8.d	See pages 223, 228 and 230 for Portfolio Activities			
M.8.e	See pages 227 and 230 for Portfolio Activities			
M.8.f	See page 223 for Portfolio Activities			
M.8.h	See pages 223, 224, 227 and 230 for Portfolio Activities			
M.8.i	See page 227 for Portfolio Activity			
M.8.j	See below for Portfolio Activity			

M.8 Plan, implement and evaluate routines for young children

M.8.a, M.8.b, M.8.c, M.8.d, M.8.e, M.8.f, M.8.g, M.8.h, M.8.i – See grid M.8 for cross-referenced knowledge based activities.

M.8.j Portfolio Activity

As the officer in charge it has been brought to your notice by a parent within the workplace that another member of staff has spoken to her concerning a confidential matter relating to information confided in her, by another parent, seeking advice.

Describe how you would deal with this situation, including the member of staff involved. How would you reassure the parent that this would not arise again?

How would you approach the parent whose confidential information had been passed on, and what measures would you take to ensure that this did not happen again?

M.8.1 Plan routines for young children

<table>
<tr><th></th><th>Criteria</th><th>Knowledge evidence</th><th>Date completed</th></tr>
<tr><td rowspan="10">PROGRESS CHECKLIST</td><td>M.8.1.a</td><td>Broad knowledge of how to meet the needs of young children.</td><td></td></tr>
<tr><td>M.8.1.b</td><td>Stereotypical assumptions often made in assessing children's needs and how to avoid them.</td><td></td></tr>
<tr><td>M.8.1.c</td><td>Variations in family values and practices across cultural and other groupings and awareness that practices also vary within such groups.</td><td></td></tr>
<tr><td>M.8.1.d</td><td>Facilities available in the local community.</td><td></td></tr>
<tr><td>M.8.1.e</td><td>Contingencies and variations in routine likely to occur.</td><td></td></tr>
<tr><td>M.8.1.f</td><td>The background and previous experience of the children in the group.</td><td></td></tr>
<tr><td>M.8.1.g</td><td>When and how to involve children in planning.</td><td></td></tr>
<tr><td>M.8.1.h</td><td>How to plan within a given time frame.</td><td></td></tr>
<tr><td>M.8.1.i</td><td>The need to take account of health and safety issues when planning.</td><td></td></tr>
<tr><td>M.8.1.j</td><td>The role that other workers play in providing an overall framework for routine planning.</td><td></td></tr>
</table>

USEFUL BOOKS

Your assessor will have details of suitable reading material for this unit.

PORTFOLIO ACTIVITY SUMMARY				
Criteria	**Portfolio page reference**	**0–1**	**1–4**	**4–7**
M.8.1.a, c, f, h, j	See below for Portfolio Activity			
M.8.1.d	See below for Portfolio Activity			
M.8.1.g	See page 224 for Portfolio Activity			
M.8.1.i	See page 224 for Portfolio Activity			

M.8.1.a, M.8.1.c, M.8.1.f, M.8.1.h, M.8.1.j, M.8.2.b Portfolio Activity

During a routine staff meeting within your setting it has been noted that not all of the activities are meeting individuals' needs, leading to lack of interest and inappropriate behaviour in some children.

Taking into account the previous experience of the children, family values and practices across the cultural groups, devise a routine to show activities that have been adapted and extended to meet all their needs.

M.8.1.b   State five stereotypical assumptions often made when assessing children's needs.

....

From your own experience or from your setting's routine, describe how you could avoid making them.

....

M.8.1.d Portfolio Activity

Observe the local and surrounding area of your workplace, making a note of the amenities available within the area that would be of special interest and perhaps relate to your topic/theme.

Taking into account the following headings, plan out a routine visit to one of the noted amenities:

> *(a) children's ages;*
> *(b) distance to travel;*
> *(c) costing, transport;*
> *(d) curriculum areas covered;*
> *(e) safety issues;*
> *(f) date, time of event.*

M.8.1.e   State and give reasons for the contingencies and variations in the weekly
routine that may occur.

....

How would you deal with them?

....

M.8.1.g Portfolio Activity

Look at your workplace's routine for the week, and state when it would be appropriate to involve children within a group planning session for an activity.

Implement this within your workplace, showing the time that you allocated for this on the routine of the week.

Give a full account of the procedure you followed to implement the planning session with a group of children and an evaluation of how it actually went, plus any modifications that you would make.

List the learning outcomes for the children and yourself.

M.8.1.i Portfolio Activity

State the areas within your workplace that would need to be monitored concerning health and safety.

Devise a routine checklist of items that would fit into this criteria upon a daily, two weekly, monthly, termly and yearly basis.

Plan two routines, one concerning health and one concerning safety, that would be implemented within the weekly routine, that involves the children's awareness.

M.8.2 Implement routines planned for young children

	Criteria	Knowledge evidence	Date completed
PROGRESS CHECKLIST	M.8.2.a	How to use routine activities to enhance children's learning.	
	M.8.2.b	Periods of time for which children at various stages of development are capable of sustaining concentration.	
	M.8.2.c	Methods of supporting children in the development of self-help skills.	
	M.8.2.d	The role of routine in promoting children's security and how to recognise signs of distress and insecurity.	
	M.8.2.e	How to encourage children to participate.	
	M.8.2.f	Simple record keeping techniques.	
	M.8.2.g	The health and safety requirements of the setting.	
	M.8.2.h	The need to adapt or modify planned routines to suit children's needs and interests and to capitalise on unplanned learning opportunities.	
	M.8.2.i	How to make the best use of indoor and outdoor environments in implementing plans.	
	M.8.2.j	How to use your time and the children's time effectively.	
	M.8.2.k	Where and how to obtain and use material and human resources.	
	M.8.2.l	How to use and adapt existing and readily available resources in an innovative and flexible manner.	

USEFUL BOOKS

Your assessor will have details of suitable reading material for this unit.

PORTFOLIO ACTIVITY SUMMARY				
Criteria	**Portfolio page reference**	**0–1**	**1–4**	**4–7**
M.8.2.b	See page 223 for Portfolio Activity			
M.8.2.f	See page 227 for Portfolio Activity			
M.8.2.g	See page 227 for Portfolio Activity			
M.8.2.h, i	See page 227 for Portfolio Activity			
M.8.2.k	See page 228 for Portfolio Activity			
M.8.2.l	See page 228 for Portfolio Activity			

M.8.2.a   How do the activities within your workplace's routines encourage the children's learning?

....

How could you adapt or extend the activities further, taking into consideration the level of development and concentration span of the children?

....

 ### M.8.2.b Portfolio Activity

See M.8.1.a on page 223.

M.8.2.c,   List ten self-help skills.
M.8.2.j
....

During the daily routine, when would there be an appropriate time to encourage the development of children's 'self-help skills'?

....

Describe your role as a carer within such a task.

....

M.8.2.d   Give reasons for a structured routine within the workplace.

....

From your experience and observations, state how you have recognised and dealt with a child who is distressed and insecure within such a routine.

If you have not experienced this type of situation, state how you would propose to deal with it.

....

M.8.2.e   State why it is important for the children to participate within the routine of the workplace.

....

How could you encourage children to participate within certain group activities, or to take on responsibility?

....

M.8.2.f Portfolio Activity

State how you could build simple record keeping into the routine, concerning activity areas.

List the important factors in doing so.

Draw up a sheet showing how you could monitor and record an activity area, stating how often you would carry this out and where it would fit into the routine.

M.8.2.g Portfolio Activity

Devise a booklet that would be useful to have at hand within the workplace, stating the health and safety requirements of the setting. This could be shown to staff, parents, visitors, and students upon request.

Within this booklet you could include the health and safety checklist, fire procedure, the member of staff who has the responsibility for health and safety within the setting and accident procedures.

M.8.2.h, M.8.2.i Portfolio Activity

Describe what you understand by the term 'children's needs'.

Provide a plan to show how you would adapt the workplace routine to capitalise upon the children's interests, implementing both the inside and outside environments and ensuring that their needs are being met.

M.8.2.k Portfolio Activity

You have been requested to carry out an activity which relates to your workplace's theme, but unfortunately the necessary resources and equipment are not available within the setting.

Choose one of the themes below, and decide upon a corresponding activity for which you would have to research how, where and from whom you would gather the necessary equipment and resources.

(a) Journeys
(b) Changes
(c) Families
(d) Images

Give a detailed account of how you would implement the above.

M.8.2.l Portfolio Activity

From the list below choose four activities and state ways in which you would adapt and add to them to provide a wider imaginative approach to enhance children's learning.

(a) Lego
(b) Playdough
(c) Climbing frame
(d) Paint
(e) Grassed area

(e) Home area
(f) Sand play
(g) Water play
(h) Garage
(i) Book area

M.8.3 Evaluate routines planned for young children

PROGRESS CHECKLIST	Criteria	Knowledge evidence	Date completed
	M.8.3.a	The purpose of evaluation.	
	M.8.3.b	How to set and use criteria for evaluation.	
	M.8.3.c	Methods of monitoring, observing and recording for evaluation purposes.	
	M.8.3.d	Methods of self-evaluation.	
	M.8.3.e	How to present evaluation information in suitable forms for different people/purposes.	
	M.8.3.f	How to use evaluation information in further planning.	
	M.8.3.g	How to link evaluation to children's development.	
	M.8.3.h	How to contribute to team evaluation as appropriate.	

USEFUL BOOKS

Your assessor will have details of suitable reading material for this unit.

PORTFOLIO ACTIVITY SUMMARY

Criteria	Portfolio page reference	0–1	1–4	4–7
M.8.3.a, b	See page 230 for Portfolio Activity			
M.8.3.c, f, g, h	See page 230 for Portfolio Activity			

M.8.3.a, M.8.3.b Portfolio Activity

Give reasons for the need for evaluation within the set routine of the workplace.

Research materials and documents used for evaluation purposes and prepare a report on them. State your opinion on the presentation and the criteria used for evaluation purposes.

M.8.3.c, M.8.3.f, M.8.3.g, M.8.3.h Portfolio Activity

With the permission of your placement/workplace and that of the parents/parental carers, choose four children of a similar age and carry out a checklist with them, if this is available to you, or choose a range of activities that would cover their all-round development, on a one-to-one basis, recording your findings accurately.

Compare the children's development and prepare an overall evaluation suggesting areas that may need highlighting with the aid of further activities.

Compose a proposed role play of a team planning session of four or five staff, implementing your evaluations from your baseline assessment, and the activities that you wish to implement to aid the children's development and awareness.

Include within your proposed role play how you would encourage one member of staff to see and understand your point of view.

M.8.3.d, M.8.3.e   How would you build methods of self-evaluation for both the children and yourself into the routine?

....

Suggest activities and games that would lend themselves to self-evaluation.

....

How would these activities aid you with assessing a child's development?

....

How often would you implement these activities?

....

M.2 CARRY OUT THE ADMINISTRATION OF THE PROVISION FOR A CARE/EDUCATION SETTING

	Criteria	Unit wide knowledge	Date completed
PROGRESS CHECKLIST	M.2.a	A basic understanding of methods of keeping records.	
	M.2.b	The policies and procedures of the setting concerning authorisation of expenditure.	

USEFUL BOOKS

Profiling, Recording and Observing: A Resource Pack for the Early Years. B. Stierer *et al.* (1993) Routledge.
Special Issues in Child Care. M. O'Hagan and M. Smith (1994) Bailliere Tindall.

✓ Grid M.2

Please tick box when activity is complete.
P = *Portfolio Activity*

M.2.a	M.2.2.a	M.2.2.b	M.2.2.c	M.2.2.d	M.2.2.e
	P	P	P	P	P
	M.2.3.a	M.2.3.b	M.2.3.c	M.2.3.d	
	P	P	P	P	

M.2.b	M.2.1.a	M.2.1.b	M.2.4.a	M.2.5.a
	M.2.5.b	M.2.5.c	M.2.5.d	M.2.5.e

PORTFOLIO ACTIVITY SUMMARY				
Criteria	**Portfolio page reference**	**0–1**	**1–4**	**4–7**
M.2.a	See pages 234 and 235 for Portfolio Activities			

M.2 Carry out the administration of the provision for a care/education setting

M.2.a, M.2.b – See grid M.2 for cross-referenced knowledge evidence activities.

M.2.1 Receive and disburse monies

<table>
<tr><th rowspan="2">PROGRESS CHECKLIST</th><th>Criteria</th><th>Knowledge evidence</th><th>Date completed</th></tr>
<tr><td>M.2.1.a</td><td>Methods of keeping records of income and expenditure.</td><td></td></tr>
<tr><td></td><td>M.2.1.b</td><td>The candidate's role in relation to the policies and procedures of the setting concerning:
i) authorisation of expenditure;
ii) flexibility about families' payments.</td><td></td></tr>
</table>

USEFUL BOOKS

Special Issues in Child Care. M. O'Hagan and M. Smith (1994) Bailliere Tindall (Chapter 10).

M.2.1.a,   Find out how records of income and expenditure are kept at your
M.2.4.a   workplace/placement.

....

M.2.1.b   While planning for activities at your workplace/placement you realise that you need to order more books. What is the policy/procedure for ordering new stock? Who would authorise the expenditure?

....

A parent at the private day nursery where you are working explains that he/she is unable to pay all of this month's fee due to financial difficulties. How would you deal with this situation? (Remember confidentiality.)

....

M.2.2 Implement admissions procedures

Criteria	Knowledge evidence	Date completed
M.2.2.a	Admissions policies of the setting.	
M.2.2.b	Candidate's role in relation to admissions.	
M.2.2.c	Information required about children and families.	
M.2.2.d	Information to give to parents.	
M.2.2.e	Settling-in arrangements.	

(PROGRESS CHECKLIST)

USEFUL BOOKS

Bright Ideas for Early Years: Getting Started. L. Mort and J. Morris (1989) Scholastic.

PORTFOLIO ACTIVITY SUMMARY

Criteria	Portfolio page reference	0–1	1–4	4–7
M.2.2.a, b, c, d, e	See below for Portfolio Activity			

M.2.2.a, M.2.2.b, M.2.2.c, M.2.2.d, M.2.2.e *Portfolio Activity*

Design a comprehensive information booklet which includes the following:

> *(a) admissions policy of the setting;*
> *(b) Your role in relation to admissions;*
> *(c) information required about children and their families;*
> *(d) information needed by parents/carers;*
> *(e) settling-in arrangements.*

M.2.3 Maintain records of information

Criteria	Knowledge evidence	Date completed
M.2.3.a	Methods of keeping records.	
M.2.3.b	The requirements of the registering authority for records.	
M.2.3.c	The policies of the setting concerning confidentiality.	
M.2.3.d	Information needed in an emergency.	

PROGRESS CHECKLIST

USEFUL BOOKS

Teacher Timesavers: Essentials for Everyday. Pat Gooch (1993) Scholastic.
Bright Ideas: Classroom Management. D. Montgomery and A. Rawlings (1992) Scholastic.
Communicating with Children and Adults: Interpersonal Skills for those Working with Babies and Children. P. Petrie (1989) Edward Arnold (Chapter 12: Confidentiality).

PORTFOLIO ACTIVITY SUMMARY

Criteria	Portfolio page reference	0–1	1–4	4–7
M.2.3.a, b, c, d	See below for Portfolio Activity			

M.2.3.a, M.2.3.b, M.2.3.c, M.2.3.d Portfolio Activity

Design a staff handbook which outlines the policies concerning record keeping and confidentiality in your workplace/placement. Include the following:

(a) *policy statement concerning confidentiality and record keeping;*
(b) *local authority requirements regarding records in the setting;*
(c) *sample child's personal record including emergency contact numbers, special requirements etc.;*
(d) *samples of other record sheets e.g. observation, assessment etc.*

M.2.4 Operate Budgets

	Criteria	Knowledge evidence	Date completed
PROGRESS CHECKLIST	M.2.4.a	How to record expenditure against budget limits.	

USEFUL BOOKS

Special Issues in Childcare. M. O'Hagan and M. Smith (1993) Bailliere Tindall (Chapter 10 Management Skills).

M.2.4.a   See M.2.1.a on page 233.

M.2.5 Operate systems for the supply of materials and equipment

<table>
<tr><th>PROGRESS CHECKLIST</th><th>Criteria</th><th>Knowledge evidence</th><th>Date completed</th></tr>
<tr><td></td><td>M.2.5.a</td><td>The procedures of the setting concerning ordering/hiring equipment and materials.</td><td></td></tr>
<tr><td></td><td>M.2.5.b</td><td>Suitable suppliers of relevant equipment and materials.</td><td></td></tr>
<tr><td></td><td>M.2.5.c</td><td>How to record stock levels.</td><td></td></tr>
<tr><td></td><td>M.2.5.d</td><td>How to maintain simple inventories of equipment.</td><td></td></tr>
<tr><td></td><td>M.2.5.e</td><td>Suitable and safe methods of storing different types of materials.</td><td></td></tr>
</table>

USEFUL BOOKS

Bright Ideas: Classroom Management. D. Montgomery and A. Rawlings (1992) Scholastic.

M.2.5.a   What is the procedure for ordering/hiring equipment and materials at your workplace/placement?

....

M.2.5.b   List suitable suppliers of equipment and materials appropriate for the children in your workplace/placement.

....

M.2.5.c   How do you record stock levels in your setting?

....

M.2.5.d   Outline a simple inventory of equipment.

....

M.2.5.e   List the suitable and safe methods of storing the following materials:

(*a*) powder paint
(*b*) PVA glue
(*c*) bleach
(*d*) disinfectant
(*e*) sand
(*f*) clay
(*g*) polystyrene
(*h*) felt tips
(*i*) playdough
(*j*) counters

....

P.8 ESTABLISH AND MAINTAIN ARRANGEMENTS WITH PARENTS FOR THE PROVISION OF THE CHILD-CARE SERVICE
UNIT WIDE KNOWLEDGE

——

	Criteria	Unit wide knowledge	Date completed
PROGRESS CHECKLIST	P.8.a	The central role played by parents in children's welfare and development, and the bond between children and parents.	
	P.8.b	How to communicate with parents as equals, how to listen to parents and how to adjust and modify communication with parents according to their interest, knowledge and confidence.	
	P.8.c	The social, environmental and cultural context in which local families live.	
	P.8.d	Feelings of some parents of apprehension, uncertainty or lack of confidence in relating to the candidate and the setting.	
	P.8.e	Variations in family values and practices across cultural and other groupings and awareness that practices also vary within such groups.	
	P.8.f	Sources of help when faced with difficulties in communication.	

USEFUL BOOKS

Special Issues in Child Care. M. O'Hagan and M. Smith (1994) Bailliere Tindall.
Working with Children. D. Haughton and M. McColgan (1995) Collins Educational.

✓ Grid P.8

Please tick box when activity is complete.
P = *Portfolio Activity*

P.8.a	P.8.2.b	P.8.4.a	P.8.4.c
		P	

P.8.b	P.8.1.d	P.8.4.b	P.8.2.e

P.8.c		P.8.2.d
		P

P.8.d	P.8.2.c	P.8.3.e

P.8.e	P.8.1.a	P.8.1.b	P.8.1.c
		P	P

P.8.f	P.8.2.a	P.8.3.a	P.8.3.b	P.8.3.c
		P	P	P

PORTFOLIO ACTIVITY SUMMARY				
Criteria	**Portfolio page reference**	**0–1**	**1–4**	**4–7**
P.8.a	See page 247 for Portfolio Activity			
P.8.c	See page 245 for Portfolio Activity			
P.8.e	See page 243 for Portfolio Activity			
P.8.f	See page 246 for Portfolio Activity			

Establish and maintain arrangements with parents for the provision of the child-care setting

P.8.a, P.8.b, P.8.c, P.8.d, P.8.e, P.8.f – See grid P.8 for cross-referenced knowledge based activities.

P.8.1 Identify a family's requirements for a child-care service

<table>
<tr><td rowspan="5">PROGRESS CHECKLIST</td><td>Criteria</td><td>Knowledge evidence</td><td>Date completed</td></tr>
<tr><td>P.8.1.a</td><td>How to gather information from observation of children and parents.</td><td></td></tr>
<tr><td>P.8.1.b</td><td>How to record information on family's requirements.</td><td></td></tr>
<tr><td>P.8.1.c</td><td>Other sources of information and how to evaluate its relevance for identifying the family's need.</td><td></td></tr>
<tr><td>P.8.1.d</td><td>Techniques for enabling parents to express their requirements and wishes.</td><td></td></tr>
</table>

USEFUL BOOKS

Communicating with Children and Adults: Interpersonal Skills for those Working with Babies and Children. Pat Petrie (1989) Edward Arnold.

PORTFOLIO ACTIVITY SUMMARY

Criteria	Portfolio page reference	0–1	1–4	4–7
P.8.1.b, c	See page 243 for Portfolio Activity			

P.8.1.a   Suggest three pieces of information that you may be able to gather from observation of children and parents.

....

Suggest one method of gathering this information.

....

P.8.1.b, P.8.1.c Portfolio Activity

Design a sheet on which you can record information on a family's requirements. You will need to include all your sources of information and suggest how relevant each one has been for identifying the family's need.

P.8.1.d, P.8.2.e	Suggest three techniques you may have used or may use for enabling parents to express their requirements and wishes.

P.8.2 Negotiate arrangements for the provision of child care with parents

	Criteria	Knowledge evidence	Date completed
PROGRESS CHECKLIST	P.8.2.a	The extent of the service available and the degree of flexibility within it.	
	P.8.2.b	The importance and value of parents' knowledge about their children.	
	P.8.2.c	The negative feelings some parents have about other people caring for their children.	
	P.8.2.d	The conflicting pressures of family and work roles on some parents.	
	P.8.2.e	Techniques for enabling parents to seek clarification and ask questions.	

USEFUL BOOKS

Bright Ideas: Classroom Management. D. Montgomery and A. Rawlings (1992) Scholastic.

PORTFOLIO ACTIVITY SUMMARY				
Criteria	Portfolio page reference	0–1	1–4	4–7
P.8.2.d	See page 245 for Portfolio Activity			

P.8.2.a   Within your workplace/setting find out the extent of the service available and the degree of flexibility within it.

....

P.8.2.b   List five reasons why it is essential for people who work with children to value parents' knowledge about their own children.

....

P.8.2.c   Why might some parents have negative feelings about other people caring for their children? Give your ideas.

....

P.8.2.d Portfolio Activity

Research the conflicting pressures of family and work roles on some parents. Present your findings in the form of a short report.

P.8.2.e   See P.8.1.d on page 243.

P.8.3 Establish and maintain agreements with parents

<table>
<tr><td rowspan="4">PROGRESS CHECKLIST</td><td>**Criteria**</td><td>**Knowledge evidence**</td><td>**Date completed**</td></tr>
<tr><td>P.8.3.a</td><td>The implications of written agreements.</td><td></td></tr>
<tr><td>P.8.3.b</td><td>Sources of legally tested formats of agreements.</td><td></td></tr>
<tr><td>P.8.3.c</td><td>The importance of regular review of written agreements.</td><td></td></tr>
</table>

USEFUL BOOKS

Special Issues in Child Care. M. O'Hagan and M. Smith (1994) Bailliere Tindall.
Bright Ideas: Classroom Management. D. Montgomery and A. Rawlings (1992) Scholastic.

PORTFOLIO ACTIVITY SUMMARY

Criteria	Portfolio page reference	0–1	1–4	4–7
P.8.3.a, b, c	See below for Portfolio Activity			

 ### P.8.3.a, P.8.3.b, P.8.3.c Portfolio Activity

Research the implications of written agreements and where possible locate some legally tested formats of agreements. Design a format for all written agreements that you could use with parents which would be appropriate for your workplace/placement. For example, parental involvement in a behaviour modification programme or parental agreement to abide by the rules of a private day nursery. State in your format how often you will review this agreement.

P.8.4 Establish and maintain exchange of information with parents about the care of their children

<table>
<tr><td rowspan="4" style="writing-mode:vertical-lr">PROGRESS CHECKLIST</td><td>**Criteria**</td><td>**Knowledge evidence**</td><td>**Date completed**</td></tr>
<tr><td>P.8.4.a</td><td>Parents' need for regular information about their children in order to sustain continuity of care.</td><td></td></tr>
<tr><td>P.8.4.b</td><td>The policy of the setting concerning confidentiality and the importance of safeguarding confidentiality of information.</td><td></td></tr>
<tr><td>P.8.4.c</td><td>Key indicators of the sequence of child development 6 weeks to 8 years, including normal and deviations from normal relative to background.</td><td></td></tr>
</table>

USEFUL BOOKS

Teacher Timesavers. Pat Gooch (1993) Scholastic.
Babies and Young Children Book 1 – Development 0–7. Beaver *et al.* (1994) Stanley Thornes.
Communicating with Children and Adults: Interpersonal Skills for those Working with Babies and Children. Pat Petrie (1989) Edward Arnold.

PORTFOLIO ACTIVITY SUMMARY				
Criteria	**Portfolio page reference**	**0–1**	**1–4**	**4–7**
P.8.4.a	See below for Portfolio Activity			

 ### P.8.4.a Portfolio Activity

Design a programme that will cater for parents' needs with regard to receiving regular information about their children.

P.8.4.b   Find out about the policy of your workplace/placement concerning confidentiality.

Give reasons why it is important to safeguard confidentiality of information.

P.8.4.c   Find out the most widely used development checklists.

....

Why do child care workers use developmental checklists?

....

P.3 INVOLVE PARENTS IN PLAY AND OTHER LEARNING ACTIVITIES WITH YOUNG CHILDREN

PROGRESS CHECKLIST

Criteria	Unit wide knowledge	Date completed
P.3.a	How to communicate with parents as equals, how to listen to parents and how to adjust and modify communications with parents according to their interest, knowledge and confidence about participating in children's activities.	
P.3.b	The social, environmental and cultural context in which local families live.	

USEFUL BOOKS

Your assessor will have details of suitable reading material for this unit.

✓ Grid P.3

Please tick box when activity is complete.

P = *Portfolio Activity*

P.3.a	P.3.1.a	P.3.1.b	P.3.1.c	P.3.1.d	P.3.1.e	P.3.2.a	P.3.2.b
	P.3.2.d	P.3.2.e	P.3.2.f	P3.2.g	P.3.3.a	P.3.3.b	P.3.3.c

P.3.b	P.3.2.c	P.3.2.h

P.3 Involve parents in play and other learning activities with young children

P.3.a, P.3.b – See grid P.3 for cross-referenced knowledge based activities.

P.3.1 Share information with parents about adults' involvement in children's activities

PROGRESS CHECKLIST

Criteria	Knowledge evidence	Date completed
P.3.1.a	The value of parental involvement for children and parents.	
P.3.1.b	How to create a suitable environment for sharing of information with parents.	
P.3.1.c	The value and purposes of the children's activities/experiences and knowing how to communicate this to parents.	
P.3.1.d	How to share information with parents.	
P.3.1.e	The variety of ways in which parents can be involved in children's activities and the importance of negotiating their type and level of involvement.	

USEFUL BOOKS

Communicating with Children and Adults: Interpersonal Skills for those Working with Babies and Children. P. Petrie (1989) Edward Arnold.

P.3.1.a   State the value of parental involvement for both children and parents.

....

P.3.1.b   Describe how you would create a suitable environment for sharing information with parents.

....

P.3.1.c,   Describe the value and purposes of the children's activities/experiences.
P.3.1.d

....

How would you communicate these to parents?

P.3.1.e   Suggest five questions that parents may propose to you concerning play and learning activities.

....

How would you respond to each in a positive manner?

....

List ways in which parents can be involved in children's activities.

....

Describe the importance of negotiating the parents' type and level of involvement.

....

P.3.2 Encourage parents to become involved in children's activities

	Criteria	Knowledge evidence	Date completed
PROGRESS CHECKLIST	P.3.2.a	Awareness of some parents' feelings of lack of skills or embarrassment at joining in children's activities.	
	P.3.2.b	How to create a welcoming atmosphere for parents.	
	P.3.2.c	Why some parents may have limits to the extent of their involvement and should not be subject to pressure to be involved beyond these limits.	
	P.3.2.d	The most appropriate way to involve parents.	
	P.3.2.e	Understand that the child care worker is likely to be seen as a role model by parents.	
	P.3.2.f	The purpose of children's activities and the adults' role in them.	
	P.3.2.g	Ways/techniques of involving parents at a practical level.	
	P.3.2.h	The cultural background which influences parents' wishes and needs.	

USEFUL BOOKS

Communicating with Children and Adults: Interpersonal Skills for those Working with Babies and Children. P. Petrie (1989) Edward Arnold.

P.3.2.a,
P.3.2.d,
P.3.2.g

State how parents may feel about joining in with children's activities.

....

Describe ways/techniques of involving parents at a practical level, bearing in mind their feelings.

....

State the most appropriate ways of involving individual parents.

....

P.3.2.b   State how you would create a welcoming atmosphere for parents.

....

P.3.2.c   Suggest why some parents may have limits to the extent of their involvement.

....

How would you ensure that you do not put undue pressure upon parents to be involved beyond these limits?

....

P.3.2.e   Describe how you would ensure that you, as a child care worker, are observed by parents as a good role model.

....

P.3.2.f   Describe the purpose of children's activities and the adults' role in them.

....

P.3.2.h   Suggest how the cultural background of parents may influence their wishes and views.

....

P.3.3 Provide feedback to parents about their involvement in children's activities

PROGRESS CHECKLIST

Criteria	Knowledge evidence	Date completed
P.3.3.a	Different ways of giving and receiving feedback which could assist further parental involvement.	
P.3.3.b	The need to make time and space for parents to give and receive feedback.	
P.3.3.c	How parents' involvement in children's activities can benefit parents themselves.	

USEFUL BOOKS

Between Ourselves: An Introduction to Interpersonal Communication. G. Burton and R. Dimbleby (1992) Edward Arnold.

P.3.3.a   List various ways in which you could give feedback and receive it, which in turn could assist further parental involvement.

....

P.3.3.b   How would you ensure that you made time and space for parents to give and receive feedback?

....

P.3.3.c   Describe how a parent's involvement within children's activities can be of benefit for him or herself.

....

P.5 INVOLVE PARENTS IN A GROUP FOR YOUNG CHILDREN

UNIT WIDE KNOWLEDGE

PROGRESS CHECKLIST	Criteria	Unit wide knowledge	Date completed
	P.5.a	The organisation of the group.	
	P.5.b	The benefits to the group, the parents and the children of parents' involvement in the group.	
	P.5.c	How to communicate with parents as equals, how to listen to parents and how to adjust and modify communication with parents according to their interest, knowledge and confidence in the group.	
	P.5.d	Awareness of the circumstances and pressures which affect parents' lives and consequently their involvement in the group including the apprehension often felt by parents on coming into a new situation, and ways of supporting them as they adjust.	
	P.5.e	The social, environmental and cultural context in which local families live.	
	P.5.f	Awareness that values and practices differ within cultural and other groups as well as across such groups.	

USEFUL BOOKS

People in Organisations. E. Sallis and K. Sallis (1990) Macmillan.
Working with Children. D. Houghton and M. McColgan (1995) Collins Educational.
Communicating with Children and Adults: Interpersonal Skills for those Working with Babies and Children. P. Petrie (1989) Edward Arnold.

Grid P.5

Please tick box when activity is complete.

P = *Portfolio Activity*

P.5.a	P.5.3.c	P.5.4.d

P.5.b	P.5.2.a	P.5.4.a	P.5.4.b	P.5.4.c

P.5.c	P.5.1.a	P.5.1.b	P.5.1.c	P.5.1.d	P.5.1.e	P.5.3.a
	P	P	P			

P.5.d	P.5.2.b	P.5.2.c	P.5.2.d	P.5.4.e
	P	P	P	

P.5.e	P.5.3.b
	P

P.5.f	P.5.4.f

PORTFOLIO ACTIVITY SUMMARY				
Criteria	**Portfolio page reference**	**0–1**	**1–4**	**4–7**
P.5.c	See page 259 for Portfolio Activity			
P.5.d	See page 261 for Portfolio Activity			
P.5.e	See page 263 for Portfolio Activity			

P.5 Involve parents in a group for young children

P.5.a, P.5.b, P.5.c, P.5.d, P.5.e, P.5.f – See grid P.5 for cross-referenced knowledge evidence activities.

P.5.1 Inform parents about the group

PROGRESS CHECKLIST	Criteria	Knowledge evidence	Date completed
	P.5.1.a	A variety of methods of communication appropriate to members of the local community and how to gain access to their use.	
	P.5.1.b	How to present information in lively, interesting and welcoming ways.	
	P.5.1.c	Information and advice commonly sought by parents.	
	P.5.1.d	Other people or agencies able to provide information and advice.	
	P.5.1.e	The boundaries of responsibility for work with parents and to whom enquiries beyond these should be referred.	

USEFUL BOOKS

Communicating with Children and Adults: Interpersonal Skills for those Working with Babies and Children. P. Petrie (1989) Edward Arnold.
Between Ourselves: An Introduction to Interpersonal Communication. G. Burton and R. Dimbleby (1992) Edward Arnold.
People in Organisations. E. Sallis and K. Sallis (1990) Macmillan.

PORTFOLIO ACTIVITY SUMMARY

Criteria	Portfolio page reference	0–1	1–4	4–7
P.5.1.a, b, c	See below for Portfolio Activity			

P.5.1.a, P.5.1.b, P.5.1.c Portfolio Activity

Design a poster for children and parents which outlines the facilities available in your type of setting in an interesting and welcoming way.

Design a leaflet which could be distributed in the local community which provides information and advice about the setting.

P.5.1.d   List other people or agencies who might provide relevant information and advice to parents who make use of the facilities at your workplace/placement.

....

P.5.1.e   Give two examples of when you would need to refer parents to other professionals.

....

P.5.2 Encourage parents to attend the group

PROGRESS CHECKLIST	Criteria	Knowledge evidence	Date completed
	P.5.2.a	Ways of encouraging parents and carers to share experiences with each other.	
	P.5.2.b	Barriers, real or felt, to parents' attendance at the group.	
	P.5.2.c	Sources of assistance or strategies for helping parents to attend the group.	
	P.5.2.d	Understanding of likelihood of families' negative feelings about the group where attendance is not optional.	

USEFUL BOOKS

Working with Children. D. Haughton and M. McColgan (1995) Collins Educational.
People in Organisations. E. Sallis and K. Sallis (1990) Macmillan.
Special Issues in Child Care. M. O'Hagan and M. Smith (1994) Bailliere Tindall.

PORTFOLIO ACTIVITY SUMMARY				
Criteria	Portfolio page reference	0–1	1–4	4–7
P.5.2.b, c, d	See below for Portfolio Activity			

P.5.2.a   List four ways in which parents and carers could be encouraged to share experiences with each other.

....

 ## P.5.2.b, P.5.2.c, P.5.2.d Portfolio Activity

Devise an induction programme for children starting at your setting which might help to allay any fears the parents may have and help them and their children to adjust to the new setting.

P.5.3 Establish and maintain relationships with parents in the group

	Criteria	Knowledge evidence	Date completed
PROGRESS CHECKLIST	P.5.3.a	The policy of the group concerning confidentiality, and understanding the importance of safeguarding confidentiality of information.	
	P.5.3.b	Sources of help in cases where other languages are involved.	
	P.5.3.c	The boundaries of responsibility for work with parents and to whom other requests should be referred.	

USEFUL BOOKS

Communicating with Children and Adults: Interpersonal Skills for those Working with Babies and Children. P. Petrie (1989) Edward Arnold.
Special Educational Needs. ed. R. Gulliford and G. Upton (1992) Routledge.
Children with Special Needs: A Guide for Parents and Carers. R. Woolfson (1991) Faber and Faber.

PORTFOLIO ACTIVITY SUMMARY

Criteria	Portfolio page reference	0–1	1–4	4–7
P.5.3.b	See page 263 for Portfolio Activity			

P.5.3.a   Find out about the policy regarding confidentiality at your workplace/placement. List the key points of the policy.

....

Why is it important to maintain confidentiality when working with children?

....

P.5.3.b Portfolio Activity

Design a factsheet which outlines to parents and carers the sources of help available regarding community languages. If possible, provide a translation of the factsheet in a community language relevant to your workplace/placement. (If appropriate, you could ask a parent or member of staff to help you with the translation or you may use more than one language yourself.)

P.5.3.c   List your responsibilities towards parents in your workplace/placement.

....

To whom might you refer parents if their child had the following:

(*a*) speech problem;

....

(*b*) challenging behaviour;

....

(*c*) poor attendance;

....

(*d*) low concentration;

....

(*e*) reading difficulties.

....

P.5.4 Encourage parents to participate in the group

<table>
<tr><td rowspan="7" style="writing-mode: vertical-rl">PROGRESS CHECKLIST</td><td>**Criteria**</td><td>**Knowledge evidence**</td><td>**Date completed**</td></tr>
<tr><td>P.5.4.a</td><td>Different ways in which parents can participate in the group.</td><td></td></tr>
<tr><td>P.5.4.b</td><td>Ways in which parents' skill can help the group.</td><td></td></tr>
<tr><td>P.5.4.c</td><td>Different ways of stimulating parents' interest to participate in the group.</td><td></td></tr>
<tr><td>P.5.4.d</td><td>The nature and purpose of children's activities.</td><td></td></tr>
<tr><td>P.5.4.e</td><td>The reasons why some parents are reluctant to participate in children's activities.</td><td></td></tr>
<tr><td>P.5.4.f</td><td>How to recognise and challenge prejudice and discrimination and how to support those who are the object of it and those who perpetrate it.</td><td></td></tr>
</table>

USEFUL BOOKS

Special Issues in Child Care. M. O'Hagan and M. Smith (1994) Bailliere Tindall.
Working with Children. D. Haughton and M. McColgan (1995) Collins Educational.
The Early Years: Laying the Foundations for Racial Equality. I. Sirjai-Bletchford (1994) Trentham Books.
53 Interesting Ways to Promote Equal Opportunities in Education. V. Lewis and S. Habeshaw (1990) Technical and Educational Services.

P.5.4.a,   List four ways in which parents can be encouraged to participate in your
P.5.4.c   group setting.

....

P.5.4.b   How can parents be encouraged to use their skills to help the group setting?

....

P.5.4.d   Draw a spidergram which illustrates how and why children's play activities are an essential element of their learning.

....

List two ways in which parents can provide support for children's learning through play activities.

....

P.5.4.e   Give reasons why parents might be reluctant to participate in children's activities in the setting.

....

P.5.4.f   What would you do if a parent made a racist remark whilst working with a group of children?

....

How would you support the person who was the object of such a remark?

....

What steps could you take to challenge prejudice and discrimination from parents or children with whom you work?

....

C.17 CONTRIBUTE TO THE CARE AND EDUCATION OF CHILDREN WITH SPECIAL NEEDS UNIT WIDE KNOWLEDGE

PROGRESS CHECKLIST	Criteria	Unit wide knowledge	Date completed
	C.17.a	The overall course of children's development.	
	C.17.b	Awareness of the implications of physical, intellectual and sensory impairment and how these affect the development of children.	
	C.17.c	How to assess the individual child's level of development in context.	
	C.17.d	The roles, expertise and different perspectives of the various professionals involved with children with special needs.	
	C.17.e	How to liaise with other agencies.	
	C.17.f	Where to obtain specific information relating to special needs and associated services.	
	C.17.g	Working knowledge of the legislation which covers both education and care provision for children with special needs.	
	C.17.h	The support network for families with children with special needs.	

Useful books

Babies and Young Children Book 1 – Development 0–7. Beaver *et al.* (1994) Stanley Thornes.
The Developing Child. H. Bee (1992) Harper Collins.
Special Issues in Child Care. M. O'Hagan and M. Smith (1994) Bailliere Tindall.
Primary Schools and Special Needs: Policy, Planning and Provision. S. Wolfendale (1992) Cassell.
Children with Special Needs: A Guide for Parents and Carers. R. Woolfson (1991) Faber and Faber.
Signposts to Special Needs. ed. M. Peter (1991) National Children's Bureau/NES Arnold.

✓ Grid C.17

Please tick box when activity is complete.

P = *Portfolio Activity*

C.17.a	C.17.1.a	C.17.4.a
	P	P

C.17.b	C.17.1.e	C.17.1.g	C.17.4.b

C.17.c	C.17.1.b	C.17.1.c	C.17.1.d	C.17.2.d	C.17.3.g
	P	P	P		

C.17.d	C.17.1.f	C.17.2.c

C.17.e	C.17.5.e	C.17.5.d
	P	P

C.17.f	C.17.1.h	C.17.3.a	C.17.3.b	C.17.3.c	C.17.3.d
	P	P	P	P	P
	C.17.3.e	C.17.3.f	C.17.4.c	C.17.4.d	C.17.4.e
	P	P			P

C.17.g	C.17.2.i	C.17.5.a	C.17.5.b	C.17.5.c
	P	P	P	

C.17.h	C.17.2.a	C.17.2.b	C.17.2.e	C.17.2.f	C.17.2.g	C.17.2.h	C.17.4.f

PORTFOLIO ACTIVITY SUMMARY				
Criteria	**Portfolio page reference**	**0–1**	**1–4**	**4–7**
C.17.a	See pages 271 and 280 for Portfolio Activities			
C.17.c	See page 271 for Portfolio Activity			
C.17.e	See page 282 for Portfolio Activity			
C.17.f	See pages 278 and 280 for Portfolio Activities			
C.17.g	See pages 276 and 282 for Portfolio Activities			

C.17 Contribute to the care and education of children with special needs

C.17.a, C.17.b, C.17.c, C.17.d, C.17.e, C.17.f, C.17.g, C.17.h – See grid C.17 for cross-referenced knowledge evidence activities.

C.17.1 Enable children with special needs to participate in activities

	Criteria	Knowledge evidence	Date completed
PROGRESS CHECKLIST	C.17.1.a	The range of activities and their potential in terms of child development.	
	C.17.1.b	How to select and plan appropriate activities.	
	C.17.1.c	How to select goals linked to activities and individual progress.	
	C.17.1.d	The individual child's need for support and independence.	
	C.17.1.e	The individual child's need for support and independence.	
	C.17.1.f	Methods of encouragement and support.	
	C.17.1.g	The links between effort, failure and achievement and self-confidence and self-esteem.	
	C.17.1.h	Where and how to obtain information and skills related to special equipment and its use.	

USEFUL BOOKS

From Birth to Five Years. M. Sheridan (1987) NFER Nelson.
A Practical Guide to Activities for Young Children. C. Hobart and J. Frankel (1994) Stanley Thornes.
Playing Together: Integrating Children with Special Needs into Pre-school Groups. Brady *et al.* (1994) Wales Pre-School Playgroups Association.
Children with Special Needs – A Guide for Parents and Carers. R. Woolfson (1991) Faber and Faber.
Creative Play. D. Einon (1986) Penguin.
Play with a Purpose for the Under Sevens. E. Matterson (1989) Penguin.

PORTFOLIO ACTIVITY SUMMARY

Criteria	Portfolio page reference	0–1	1–4	4–7
C.17.1.a	See below for Portfolio Activity			
C.17.1.b, c, d	See below for Portfolio Activity			
C.17.1.h	See page 278 for Portfolio Activity			

 ## C.17.1.a Portfolio Activity

Devise appropriate activities to encourage children's potential in each of the following areas:

> (a) *physical development;*
> (b) *intellectual development;*
> (c) *emotional development;*
> (d) *social development.*

Record your work using the following format for each activity:

> (i) *title;*
> (ii) *date;*
> (iii) *setting;*
> (iv) *details of children e.g. age, special needs, etc.;*
> (v) *purpose of activity;*
> (vi) *learning outcomes for children in relevant areas of physical, intellectual, social and emotional development;*
> (vii) *learning outcomes for students;*
> (viii) *implementation;*
> (ix) *evaluation;*
> (x) *modifications (including any for children with special needs).*

 ## C.17.1.b, C.17.1.c, C.17.1.d Portfolio Activity

Special Needs Observation
To be carried out in special needs placement or with a child with special needs in your workplace.

Please remember the importance of confidentiality.

*Before you begin your observation, compile a **profile of placement/workplace**. This should include such details as:*

- *situation of placement/workplace;*
- *description of establishment e.g. size, age, number of floors, type, etc.;*
- *staff e.g. number, profession etc.;*

- *children e.g. age group, range of special needs etc.;*
- *visiting specialists e.g. speech therapists etc.;*
- *parental involvement.*

The description of your work area could include:

- *plan of layout;*
- *age range of children;*
- *number of children;*
- *variety of special needs;*
- *staffing.*

The Observation

You will need to discuss with the placement supervisor which children are the most appropriate for you to observe. Please remember that there may be reasons, that only the placement supervisor may know about, for you not to observe certain children. It may not always be possible to fully discuss the reasons for this.

When a child has been chosen try to find out as much about him/her as possible.

Description of child: *Under this heading give:*

- *a description of physical appearance;*
- *an outline of special needs;*
- *an outline of overall development to date.*

Setting: *Describe the immediate setting e.g. play area, equipment involved, activity.*

Observation: *Write observation in the usual way and in great detail (remember to keep in mind the purpose of your observation).* **Be objective. Remember confidentiality.**

Evaluation

Keep in mind any special need that the child may have. Depending on the special needs of the child it may not be appropriate to compare his/her development with the same age range, children with similar special needs etc. You may be able to discuss this with your supervisor/colleagues, read appropriate books etc.

Personal Learning

This observation is an extremely valuable learning experience for you. Think and write about the following:

(a) *What have you learned from studying this child that you did not know before?*
(b) *Can you make any suggestions as to how the development of this child could be made to progress?*

Bibliography

A detailed bibliography should be included.

Special Needs Activity Plan

Use your observation to plan an activity relevant to one aspect of the child's development.

C.17.1.e,   Describe one way you have provided support for a child with special needs.
C.17.1.g   Suggest possible modifications.

....

Describe one way you have encouraged a child with special needs. Suggest possible modifications.

....

C.17.1.f   Think about the toys you already have in your workplace/placement. Choose one which would be particularly useful for providing encouragement and support for a child with one of the following:

(*a*) physical disability;
(*b*) visual impairment (blind or partially sighted);
(*c*) hearing impairment (profoundly deaf or hearing impairment);
(*d*) communication difficulty.

....

What particular developmental areas would this toy be useful for e.g. communication, thinking, movement (gross or fine) social mixing etc.?

....

Would you need to adapt this toy? How could you do this?

....

Would a specialist toy be better?

....

(**Adapted from** *Playing Together*, Bardy *et al.* (1994))

C.17.1.h Portfolio Activity

See C.17.3.a on page 278.

C.17.2 Work jointly with parents in understanding and responding to the special needs of their children

PROGRESS CHECKLIST	Criteria	Knowledge evidence	Date completed
	C.17.2.a	The central role played by parents in their children's welfare and development and the bond between children and parents.	
	C.17.2.b	How to communicate with parents as equals, how to listen to parents and how to adjust and modify communication with parents according to their interest, knowledge and confidence.	
	C.17.2.c	The candidate's role and responsibilities with regard to parents and the circumstances in which parents should be referred to senior colleagues or other professionals.	
	C.17.2.d	The importance and value of parents' knowledge and expertise concerning their children.	
	C.17.2.e	The types of information and skills needed by parents and how to communicate them effectively.	
	C.17.2.f	The social, environmental and cultural context in which local families live.	
	C.17.2.g	Variations in family values and practices across cultural and other groupings and awareness that practices also vary within such groupings.	
	C.17.2.h	The strong emotions felt by parents about their children with special needs and how to respond with sensitivity to expressions of such feelings.	
	C.17.2.i	Broad background knowledge of current medical, educational and other technical terminology associated with different types of special needs.	

USEFUL BOOKS

Children with Special Needs: A Guide for Parents and Carers. R. Woolfson (1991) Faber and Faber.
Signposts to Special Needs. ed. M. Peter (1991) National Children's Bureau/NES Arnold.
Babies and Young Children Book 1 – Development 0–7. Beaver *et al.* (1994) Stanley Thornes.
Special Parents. B. Furneaux (1988) Open University Press.
Playing Together: Integrating Children with Special Needs into Pre-School Groups. Brady *et al.* (1994) Wales Pre-School Playgroups Association.
Caring for Children: A Textbook for Nursery Nurses. P. Geraghty (1994) Bailliere Tindall (Chapters 6 and 9).

PORTFOLIO ACTIVITY SUMMARY		0–1	1–4	4–7
Criteria	**Portfolio page reference**			
C.17.2.i	See page 276 for Portfolio Activity			

C.17.2.a,   Look at the way your workplace/placement introduces children into the group
C.17.2.b   or class. How might this be adapted to cater for children with special needs and their families?

....

C.17.2.c   From your studies and/or your own experiences in the workplace/placement (but remember confidentiality) give examples of the circumstances in which parents should be referred to:

(*a*) senior colleagues;

....

(*b*) other professionals.

....

C.17.2.d   List five ways in which parents' knowledge and expertise can be valued and used to their children's advantage. Think particularly about children with special needs.

....

C.17.2.f,   When working with children with special needs it is important to take into
C.17.2.g,   account the social, environmental and cultural context in which their families

C.17.2.h   live. You need to be aware of differing family values and cultural practices and be sensitive to parents' emotions concerning their children with special needs.

List three possible social, environmental and cultural factors which may affect a family's attitudes towards special needs.

....

Give one example of how to respond to a parent's strong feelings about their child's special need. If appropriate, outline a method you have used at your workplace/placement, but remember confidentiality.

....

 ### *C.17.2.i Portfolio Activity*

Using the books suggested and other relevant sources compile a factsheet on one *type of special need using current medical, educational and other technical terminology.*

C.17.3 Contribute to the use of specialist equipment

PROGRESS CHECKLIST	Criteria	Knowledge evidence	Date completed
	C.17.3.a	A broad background knowledge of the range of specialist equipment commonly used by children with different types of special needs.	
	C.17.3.b	Where to obtain additional information on the range, use and availability of specialist equipment.	
	C.17.3.c	The policies and procedures of the setting for the supply, use, maintenance and disposal of specialist equipment.	
	C.17.3.d	How and when specific equipment should be used by the children in the setting and the reasons for their use.	
	C.17.3.e	How to help children to contribute to the management of their own aids.	
	C.17.3.f	Strategies for assisting parents in helping children with special equipment.	
	C.17.3.g	How to maintain privacy and dignity for the child.	

USEFUL BOOKS

Babies and Young Children Book 1 – Development 0–7. Beaver *et al.* (1994) Stanley Thornes.
Signposts to Special Needs. ed. M. Peter (1991) National Children's Bureau/NES Arnold.
Partially Sighted Children. Corely *et al.* (1989) NFER Nelson.
The Hearing Impaired Child. D. Goldstein (1989) NFER Nelson.
Children with Physical Disabilities. P. Halliday (1989) Cassell.
Including Pupils with Disabilities. ed. T. Booth and W. Swann (1988) Open University Press (Chapters 10, 11 and 12).

PORTFOLIO ACTIVITY SUMMARY

Criteria	Portfolio page reference	0–1	1–4	4–7
C.17.3.a, b, c, d, e, f	See below for Portfolio Activity			

 ### C.17.3.a, C.17.3.b, C.17.3.c, C.17.3.d, C.17.3.e, C.17.3.f, C.17.1.h Portfolio Activity

Using the books suggested and other relevant sources, compile a factfile on the use of special equipment in nursery/school by children with one *of the following special needs:*

(a) *cerebral palsy;*
(b) *hearing impairment;*
(c) *visual impairment.*

The factfile should cover the following areas:

(i)   *range of equipment available;*
(ii) *where it can be obtained;*
(iii) *maintenance and disposal of specialist equipment;*
(iv) *how and when used by children;*
(v)   *children's management of own aids;*
(vi) *how parents can help.*

C.17.3.g   List two reasons why confidentiality is important in relation to record keeping and assessment of children with special needs.

....

List two ways to maintain the respect and dignity of a child with special needs.

....

C.17.4 Communicate with children with special needs

PROGRESS CHECKLIST

Criteria	Knowledge evidence	Date completed
C.17.4.a	Sequence of development of language and communication in children.	
C.17.4.b	How different disabilities might hinder communication in children.	
C.17.4.c	Awareness of the range of systems of communication.	
C.17.4.d	Awareness of the validity of sign systems.	
C.17.4.e	Where to obtain information and advice on the range and use of communication aids.	
C.17.4.f	Where to obtain support for interpretation of various home languages as relevant to the local community.	

USEFUL BOOKS

Language and Reading. J. Britton (1992) Penguin.
The Education of Young Children. ed. D. Fontana (1994) Basil Blackwell.
Special Educational Needs. ed. R. Gulliford and G. Upton (1992) Routledge.
Including Pupils with Disabilities. ed. T. Booth and W. Swann (1988) Open University Press (Chapter 7 and 9.26).
Teaching the Handicapped Child. D.M. Jefferies *et al.* (1993) Souvenir Press.

PORTFOLIO ACTIVITY SUMMARY

Criteria	Portfolio page reference	0–1	1–4	4–7
C.17.4.a	See page 280 for Portfolio Activity			
C.17.4.e	See page 280 for Portfolio Activity			

C.17.4.a Portfolio Activity

See C.11.2.c, d, i and C.11.5.g on pages 129, 138.

C.17.4.b   Outline how the following disabilities might cause communication difficulties:

(*a*) autism;

....

(*b*) hearing impairment;

....

(*c*) visual impairment;

....

(*d*) Down's syndrome;

....

(*e*) cerebral palsy.

....

C.17.4.c   Outline the range of systems of communication for children with special needs.

....

C.17.4.d   British Sign Language and Makaton are two sign systems commonly used with children with special needs. Do you think that sign systems are a valid means of communicating with children with special needs? Give reasons for your answer.

....

 ### C.17.4.e Portfolio Activity

Design a leaflet giving advice and information on the range and use of communication aids relevant to one *of the following special needs:*

(*a*) *blind or visually impaired; or*
(*b*) *hearing impaired or profoundly deaf.*

C.17.4.f   Find out where to obtain support for children's home languages relevant to your own local area or placement/workplace area.

....

C.17.5 Contribute to the integration of children with special needs

	Criteria	Knowledge evidence	Date completed
PROGRESS CHECKLIST	C.17.5.a	Background knowledge of the range of provision within which children with special needs are likely to be integrated.	
	C.17.5.b	The social policy debate about integration and the legislative background to integration.	
	C.17.5.c	The policies and procedures of the agency with regard to integration.	
	C.17.5.d	How and when to share knowledge and skills with mainstream staff to assist integration.	
	C.17.5.e	The preparation that needs to be undertaken before integration takes place including the involvement of parents.	

USEFUL BOOKS

Playing Together: Integrating Children with Special Needs into Pre-School Groups. Brady *et al.* (1994) Wales Pre-School Playgroups Association.
Primary Schools and Special Needs: Policy, Planning and Provision. S. Woolfendale (1992) Cassell.
Signposts to Special Needs. ed. M. Peter (1991) National Children's Bureau/NES Arnold.
Making Sense of the Children Act 1989. N. Allen (1990) Longman (Chapter 5).
The Code of Practice on the Identification and Assessment of Special Educational Needs. (1993) Department of Education.
Meeting Special Needs in Ordinary Schools: An Overview. S. Hegarty (1989) Cassell.
Apart or A Part? Integration and the Growth of British Special Education. T. Cole (1989) Open University Press (Chapter 6).
Special Education. J. Solity (1993) Cassell (Chapter 6).

PORTFOLIO ACTIVITY SUMMARY				
Criteria	**Portfolio page reference**	**0–1**	**1–4**	**4–7**
C.17.5.a	See below for Portfolio Activity			
C.17.5.b	See below for Portfolio Activity			
C.17.5.d, e	See below for Portfolio Activity			

 ### C.17.5.a Portfolio Activity

Find out about the range of provision for children with special needs with particular reference to their integration into the mainstream. Compile a factsheet.

 ### C.17.5.b Portfolio Activity

*Using the suggested books and other relevant sources, compile a report on the process of integration as it relates to children with special needs. Include your own experiences as appropriate. Do **you** agree with the principles of integration? Give reasons for your answer.*

C.17.5.c Does your workplace/placement have a policy on integrating children with special needs?

Briefly outline their policy statement.

....

What procedures are in position for the integration of children with special needs at your workplace/placement?

....

 ### C.17.5.d, C.17.5.e Portfolio Activity

Design a leaflet (no more than four sides) outlining the benefits of pre-school provision for children with special needs and giving basic guidelines which will help groups integrate all children as fully as possible.

C.18 DEVELOP A STRUCTURED PROGRAMME FOR A CHILD WITH SPECIAL NEEDS IN PARTNERSHIP WITH PARENTS
UNIT WIDE KNOWLEDGE

Criteria	Unit wide knowledge	Date completed
C.18.a	The normal course of children's development.	
C.18.b	Awareness of the implications of physical, intellectual and sensory impairment and how these affect the development of children.	
C.18.c	The process of planning and evaluation.	
C.18.d	How to collect and analyse information on children's development and family background.	
C.18.e	Broad knowledge of the services that may be available to meet the special needs of children and their families and how to gain access to them.	
C.18.f	The importance of inter-professional working and the practical implications for the candidate's setting and role.	
C.18.g	The stress and demands on families of coping with a child with special needs.	
C.18.h	The concept of partnership with parents as equals.	
C.18.i	The boundaries of confidentiality for the setting and how, when and to whom information can be passed.	
C.18.j	Working knowledge of the legislation which covers the education and care provision for children with special needs.	

PROGRESS CHECKLIST

USEFUL BOOKS

Special Educational Needs – A Guide for Parents. (1994) Department for Education.
Code of Practice on the Identification and Assessment of Special Educational Needs. (1994) Department for Education.
Special Educational Needs. ed. R. Gulliford and G. Upton (1992) Routledge.

Grid C.18

Please tick box when activity is complete.
P = *Portfolio Activity*

C.18.a	C.18.1.e

C.18.b	C.18.3.a	C.18.3.b	C.18.3.c	C.18.3.d	C.18.3.e	C.18.3.f
	P					
	C.18.3.g	C.18.3.h	C.18.3.i	C.18.3.j	C.18.3.k	
	P	P	P	P	P	

C.18.c	C.18.2.a	C.18.2.b	C.18.2.c	C.18.5.a
		P	P	
	C.18.5.b	C.18.5.c	C.18.5.d	C.18.5.e
	P		P	P

C.18.d	C.18.1.f	C.18.5.f	C.18.1.a
	P	P	P

C.18.f	C.18.1.c

C.18.g	C.18.4.d	C.18.4.a	C.18.4.b
	P	P	P

C.18.h	C.18.4.c	C.18.1.b
		P

C.18.i	C.18.1.d

PORTFOLIO ACTIVITY SUMMARY				
Criteria	**Portfolio page reference**	**0–1**	**1–4**	**4–7**
C.18.b	See pages 293 and 294 for Portfolio Activities			
C.18.c	See pages 291 and 298 for Portfolio Activities			
C.18.d	See pages 289 and 298 for Portfolio Activities			
C.18.e	See page 287 for Portfolio Activity			
C.18.g	See pages 295 and 296 for Portfolio Activities			
C.18.h	See page 289 for Portfolio Activity			
C.18.j	See page 287 for Portfolio Activity			

C.18 Develop a structured programme for a child with special needs in partnership with parents

C.18.a, C.18.b, C.18.c, C.18.d – See grid C.18 for cross-referenced knowledge evidence activities.

C.18.e Portfolio Activity

Research the services that may be available to meet the special needs of children and their families and how to gain access to them. Present your findings in the form of a report.

C.18.f, C.18.g, C.18.h, C.18.i – See grid C.18 for cross-referenced knowledge evidence activities.

C.18.j Portfolio Activity

Research the legislation which covers the education and care provision for children with special needs. Present your findings in the form of a brief report.

C.18.1 Contribute to the assessment of a child's level of development

PROGRESS CHECKLIST	Criteria	Knowledge evidence	Date completed
	C.18.1.a	How to observe children and ways in which close observation can help identify levels of development.	
	C.18.1.b	The need for parental involvement and approval in observation and assessment and the contributions that parents can make from their extensive knowledge of their own child.	
	C.18.1.c	The roles of other professionals in regard to observations and assessments with particular reference to co-operation in assessment and confidentiality issues.	
	C.18.1.d	The policy and rules of the organisation and setting in regard to observation, assessment record keeping and confidentiality of records.	
	C.18.1.e	Stereotypical assumptions often made in assessing children's level of development and how to avoid them.	
	C.18.1.f	Outline knowledge of other methods of assessment.	

USEFUL BOOKS

A Practical Guide to Child Observation. C. Hobart and J. Frankel (1994) Stanley Thornes.

PORTFOLIO ACTIVITY SUMMARY

Criteria	Portfolio page reference	0–1	1–4	4–7
C.18.1.a	See page 289 for Portfolio Activity			
C.18.1.b	See page 289 for Portfolio Activity			
C.18.1.f	See page 289 for Portfolio Activity			

C.18.1.a Portfolio Activity

Suggest three ways of observing children and ways in which close observation can help identify levels of development. Carry out these observations and in your evaluations discuss how useful your suggestions were.

C.18.1.b Portfolio Activity

Find out how many weeks the code of practice suggests the timetable from proposing an assessment to making a statement should take. At what stage should parents become involved in the school-based stages before an assessment is made?

C.18.1.c   Study the school-based stages that schools may follow. What are the roles of the professionals involved with reference to co-operation in assessment and confidentiality issues?

(*a*) Education Service

....

(*b*) Health Service

....

(*c*) Social Services

....

C.18.1.d   Find out the policy of your organisation with regard to observation, assessment, record keeping and confidentiality.

....

C.18.1.e   Stereotypical assumptions can often be made in assessing children's level of development. Give your ideas for avoiding this.

....

C.18.1.f Portfolio Activity

Suggest five methods of assessment and give a brief outline of them e.g. ask the child to draw a person.

C.18.2 Contribute to planning a structured programme for a child

PROGRESS CHECKLIST	Criteria	Knowledge evidence	Date completed
	C.18.2.a	The organisational context for planning.	
	C.18.2.b	Ways of recording plans.	
	C.18.2.c	Methods of establishing aims and objectives in learning.	

USEFUL BOOKS

A Practical Guide to Child Observation. C. Hobart and J. Frankel (1994) Stanley Thornes.
Profiling, Recording and Observing – A Resource Pack for the Early Years. B. Steiner *et al.* (1993) Routledge.
Making Assessment Work. Drummond *et al.* (1994) NFER Nelson.

PORTFOLIO ACTIVITY SUMMARY				
Criteria	Portfolio page reference	0–1	1–4	4–7
C.18.2.b, c	See page 291 for Portfolio Activity			

C.18.2.a   Give your ideas on a daily routine.

....

C.18.2.b, C.18.2.c Portfolio Activity

An essential part of successful care/education is establishing clear aims and objectives in learning within a flexible framework of delivery. It is therefore necessary to plan and record plans effectively and clearly, and to review the work that has been implemented. Suggest a method of recording a daily plan, a weekly plan and a termly/monthly plan.

Your recording format for the termly/monthly plan should include a broad outline of topics/themes to be covered, while the weekly plan should be more specific about which activities are to be carried out during certain times of the day. Your recording of the daily plan needs to include specific aims and objectives for each activity and links with the National Curriculum, where appropriate, and method of implementation e.g. one-to-one, small group. You should include a review section to allow for recording of exactly what has been carried out and your recommendations for future work.

C.18.3 Carry out a structured activity as part of the overall programme

Criteria	Knowledge evidence	Date completed
C.18.3.a	How to provide structured activities within a group setting.	
C.18.3.b	How to communicate plans and intentions to the child in an appropriate way.	
C.18.3.c	The importance of valuing a child and communicating this.	
C.18.3.d	The need for adaptive response to the child's behaviour.	
C.18.3.e	When it is appropriate to intervene in a child's activity.	
C.18.3.f	The importance of responding to and interacting with the child.	
C.18.3.g	How to deal with contingencies and unanticipated events.	
C.18.3.h	The need for responsiveness and flexibility in implementation.	
C.18.3.i	Techniques for positive reinforcement.	
C.18.3.j	A child's need for independence, control, challenge and sense of achievement.	
C.18.3.k	Activities and strategies which enable the child and carer to have fun whilst repeating necessary exercises.	

USEFUL BOOKS

The Bright Ideas for Early Years Series. (1994) Scholastic.

PORTFOLIO ACTIVITY SUMMARY				
Criteria	**Portfolio page reference**	**0–1**	**1–4**	**4–7**
C.18.3.a	See below for Portfolio Activity			
C.18.3.g, h	See page 294 for Portfolio Activity			
C.18.3.i, j	See page 294 for Portfolio Activity			
C.18.3.k	See page 294 for Portfolio Activity			

C.18.3.a Portfolio Activity

Suggest three ways that you could provide structured activities within a group setting. Give your aims and objectives for each activity and the strategies that you will use to keep all the children on task. In these types of structured activity the role of the nursery nurse is specific. How do you see your role in this?

C.18.3.b   Communicating plans and intentions to children must be carried out in an appropriate way. List the most appropriate methods with reasons for your choice e.g. using simple language.

....

C.18.3.c,   What is the importance of valuing a child? How do you communicate this?
C.18.3.f

....

Give two reasons for the importance of responding to and interacting with the child.

....

C.18.3.d   Why is it necessary to adapt your responses to a child's changing behaviour?

....

C.18.3.e   Sometimes it may be appropriate to intervene in a child's activity. Give your views using examples from your own experience where possible.

....

 ### C.18.3.g, C.18.3.h Portfolio Activity

Recommend some strategies that you have used for dealing with contingencies and unanticipated events which demonstrate the need for responsiveness and flexibility in implementation.

 ### C.18.3.i, C.18.3.j Portfolio Activity

Describe the different techniques you have used for positive reinforcement which encourage a child's independence, control, challenge and sense of achievement.

 ### C.18.3.k Portfolio Activity

Suggest some activities and strategies you could use which will enable the child and yourself to have fun whilst repeating necessary exercises. For example Speaking and Listening Activities, *H. Mason and S. Mudd (1994) Scholastic, gives many excellent ideas for developing speaking and listening skills.*

C.18.4 Work with parents in implementing a structured programme

<table>
<tr><td rowspan="5" style="writing-mode: vertical-rl">PROGRESS CHECKLIST</td><td>**Criteria**</td><td>**Knowledge evidence**</td><td>**Date completed**</td></tr>
<tr><td>C.18.4.a</td><td>Methods of facilitating the learning of adults.</td><td></td></tr>
<tr><td>C.18.4.b</td><td>The nature of relationships within families and the importance of encouraging other family members to be actively involved with and accepting of a child with special needs.</td><td></td></tr>
<tr><td>C.18.4.c</td><td>How to communicate with parents as equals, how to listen to parents and how to adjust and modify communication with parents according to their interest, knowledge and experience.</td><td></td></tr>
<tr><td>C.18.4.d</td><td>The constraints which living conditions may impose on a parent's ability to sustain a programme.</td><td></td></tr>
</table>

USEFUL BOOKS

Special Educational Needs – A Guide for Parents. (1994) Department for Education.

PORTFOLIO ACTIVITY SUMMARY

Criteria	Portfolio page reference	0–1	1–4	4–7
C.18.4.a, b	See below for Portfolio Activity			
C.18.4.d	See page 296 for Portfolio Activity			

C.18.4.a, C.18.4.b Portfolio Activity

When working with children with special needs and their families you will not only be facilitating the learning of children but the learning of adults as well. An important aspect of your role will be encouraging other family members to be actively involved with and accepting of a child with special needs. Voluntary groups and agencies have an important role to play in this area. Research what groups and agencies exist, select three and describe the services they offer.

C.18.4.c   Consider how you and/or your colleagues communicate with parents as partners, how you/they listen to parents and how you/they adjust and modify communication with parents according to their interest, knowledge and experience.

Suggest how you might give information to parents.

....

 ### *C.18.4.d Portfolio Activity*

There may be many reasons why a parent is unable to sustain a programme at home. However, the constraints which living conditions may impose can be a serious problem e.g. a family living in poverty. Research how these constraints may affect a parent's ability to sustain a programme and give your solutions to help.

C.18.5 Contribute to the evaluation of a structured programme

Criteria	Knowledge evidence	Date completed
C.18.5.a	The purpose of evaluation.	
C.18.5.b	Methods of monitoring, observing and recording for evaluation purposes.	
C.18.5.c	How to use evaluation information in further planning.	
C.18.5.d	Methods of self-evaluation.	
C.18.5.e	Ways of identifying and measuring steps of achievement towards established aims and objectives.	
C.18.5.f	A variety of methods and formats for recording.	

USEFUL BOOKS

A Practical Guide to Child Observation. C. Hobart and J. Frankel (1994) Stanley Thornes.
'Action on Assessment', Conference Report. J. Curtis *Nursery World*, 18/5/95.
Profiling, Recording and Observing – A Resource Pack for the Early Years. B. Steiner *et al.* (1993) Routledge.
Making Assessment Work. Drummond *et al.* (1994) NFER Nelson.

PORTFOLIO ACTIVITY SUMMARY

Criteria	Portfolio page reference	0–1	1–4	4–7
C.18.5.b	See page 298 for Portfolio Activity			
C.18.5.d	See page 298 for Portfolio Activity			
C.18.5.e	See page 298 for Portfolio Activity			
C.18.5.f	See page 298 for Portfolio Activity			

C.18.5.a   What is the purpose of evaluation?

....

 ### C.18.5.b Portfolio Activity

In your placement/work setting use three methods of observing, recording and monitoring over one week for evaluation purposes. Compare the methods you have used and suggest the method which seems to be most appropriate. Remember that other people may be using your observations and evaluations and they will need to be easy to read, factual and non-judgemental.

C.18.5.c   Suggest some methods of evaluating your own performance.

....

 ### C.18.5.d Portfolio Activity

Using an evaluation you have made, take the information contained in it and use it to produce a plan for the following week's work/activities. You will need to consider your aims and objectives carefully. Take account of the learning that has already taken place and any activities that may need to be repeated. Record your plan so that all team members in the workplace will be able to share your ideas.

 ### C.18.5.e Portfolio Activity

When working towards structured aims, children often achieve part of the aims; however, if they do not complete a whole task it may appear in recording as if they achieved nothing. How can you ensure that each step is recorded and indicates they are working towards established aims and objectives?

 ### C.18.5.f Portfolio Activity

Different establishments use a variety of methods and formats for recording. Collect a sample of these formats and compare them. Which appear to be the most appropriate?

M.6 WORK WITH OTHER PROFESSIONALS
UNIT WIDE KNOWLEDGE

	Criteria	Unit wide knowledge	Date completed
PROGRESS CHECKLIST	M.6.a	A basic knowledge of the roles of other professionals in the field of child care/education.	
	M.6.b	A general basic knowledge of group dynamics.	
	M.6.c	The aims, structures and policies of own organisation.	
	M.6.d	The role of self in the organisation and the limitations of own competence and area of responsibility.	
	M.6.e	The nature of confidentiality and its boundaries.	
	M.6.f	Equal opportunities codes of practice of the organisation.	
	M.6.g	The basic principles of accountability and responsibility.	

USEFUL BOOKS

People in Organisations. E. Sallis and K. Sallis (1990) Macmillan.
Working with Children. D. Houghton and M. McColgan (1995) Collins Educational.
Special Issues in Childcare. M. O'Hagan and M. Smith (1994) Bailliere Tindall.
Children with Special Needs – A Guide for Parents and Carers. R. Woolfson (1991) Faber and Faber.
Communicating with Children and Adults: Interpersonal Skills for those Working with Babies and Children. P. Petrie (1989) Edward Arnold.

✓ Grid M.6

Please tick box when activity is complete.
P = *Portfolio Activity*

M.6.a	M.6.1.a	M.6.1.b	M.6.2.c
	P	P	P

M.6.b	M.6.1.c	M.6.3.b
		P

M.6.c	M.6.2.a
	P

M.6.d	M.6.2.b
	P

M.6.e	M.6.2.d

M.6.f	M.6.3.a
	P

M.6.g	M.6.3.c

PORTFOLIO ACTIVITY SUMMARY					
Criteria	**Portfolio page reference**	**0–1**	**1–4**	**4–7**
M.6.a	See page 302 for Portfolio Activity			
M.6.b	See page 307 for Portfolio Activity			
M.6.c	See page 305 for Portfolio Activity			
M.6.d	See page 305 for Portfolio Activity			
M.6.f	See page 305 for Portfolio Activity			

M.6 Work with other professionals

M.6.a, M.6.b, M.6.c, M.6.d, M.6.e, M.6.f, M.6.g – See grid M.6 for cross-referenced knowledge evidence activities.

M.6.1 Develop working relationships with other professionals

	Criteria	Knowledge evidence	Date completed
PROGRESS CHECKLIST	M.6.1.a	Contacts with other professionals already established by own organisation.	
	M.6.1.b	Sources of information about other relevant professionals in the locality.	
	M.6.1.c	Barriers to communication with other professionals.	

USEFUL BOOKS

Special Educational Needs. R. Gulliford and G. Upton (1992) Routledge.
Children with Special Needs – A Guide for Parents and Carers. R. Woolfson (1991) Faber and Faber.
Special Issues in Childcare. M. O'Hagan and M. Smith (1994) Bailliere Tindall.
People in Organisations. E. Sallis and K. Sallis (1990) Macmillan.
Working with Children. D. Houghton and M. McColgan (1995) Collins Educational.
Communicating with Children and Adults: Interpersonal Skills for those Working with Babies and Children. P. Petrie (1989) Edward Arnold.
Between Ourselves: An Introduction to Interpersonal Communication. G. Burton and R. Dimbleby (1992) Edward Arnold.

PORTFOLIO ACTIVITY SUMMARY

Criteria	Portfolio page reference	0–1	1–4	4–7
M.6.1.a, b	See below for Portfolio Activity			

M.6.1.a, M.6.1.b, M.6.2.c Portfolio Activity

Compile an information booklet which includes the following:

    (a) *links with other professionals established by your colleagues at work/placement;*
    (b) *where to obtain information concerning other professionals in the local area;*
    (c) *a diagram which illustrates how you and your colleagues together with other professionals function as a multi-disciplinary network.*

M.6.1.c What is the difference between a team and a network?

....

How do teams affect team members and group morale?

....

How can workers make a more effective contribution to their team?

....

List possible barriers to communication with other professionals in a network.

....

(**Adapted from** Houghton and McColgan, 1995; p. 110.)

M.6.2 Share information and skills with other professionals

<table>
<tr><td rowspan="5" style="background:black;color:white">PROGRESS CHECKLIST</td><td>Criteria</td><td>Knowledge evidence</td><td>Date completed</td></tr>
<tr><td>M.6.2.a</td><td>Systems and methods of sharing information and skills.</td><td></td></tr>
<tr><td>M.6.2.b</td><td>How to identify expertise of others which could assist own work.</td><td></td></tr>
<tr><td>M.6.2.c</td><td>Multi-disciplinary networks.</td><td></td></tr>
<tr><td>M.6.2.d</td><td>The policy of the organisation concerning confidentiality of information.</td><td></td></tr>
</table>

USEFUL BOOKS

People in Organisations. E. Sallis and K. Sallis (1990) Macmillan.
Working with Children. D. Houghton and M. McColgan (1995) Collins Educational.
Communicating with Children and Adults: Interpersonal Skills for those Working with Babies and Children. P. Petrie (1989) Edward Arnold.
The Early Years: Laying the Foundations for Racial Equality. I. Sirjai-Bletchford (1994) Trentham Books.
53 Interesting Ways to Promote Equal Opportunities in Education. V. Lewis and S. Habeshaw (1990) Technical and Educational Series.

PORTFOLIO ACTIVITY SUMMARY

Criteria	Portfolio page reference	0–1	1–4	4–7
M.6.2.a	See page 305 for Portfolio Activity			
M.6.2.b	See page 305 for Portfolio Activity			
M.6.2.c	See page 302 for Portfolio Activity			

M.6.2.a Portfolio Activity

Find out about the equal opportunities policy at your workplace/placement. Does it include information concerning children with disabilities or learning difficulties? Is there a separate policy for special needs? What are its main aims?

Find out who is responsible for co-ordinating support for children with special needs in your workplace/placement.

How would you share information about your concerns over a child with special needs? **Remember confidentiality.**

M.6.2.b, M.6.3.a Portfolio Activity

Think about your workplace/placement e.g. leadership style, gender and age mix. If possible, make a list of colleagues' posts, roles and responsibilities (do not use full names). Note any skills which staff have in relation to special needs.

List your own role and responsibilities within the workplace/placement. List the limitations of your role e.g. as a student nursery nurse or junior/unqualified member of staff.

Compile a separate list of staff members and map out who relates to whom. You could use broken lines to indicate little contact between individuals and unbroken lines to suggest close relationships.

Is there any overlap in team roles and responsibilities or skills? Give examples.

Have you noticed any previously unidentified expertise in yourself or other staff in relation to working with children with special needs? Give examples. **Remember confidentiality.**

*(**Adapted from** Houghton and McColgan, 1995, p. 111.)*

M.6.2.c Portfolio Activity

See M.6.1.a on page 302.

See M.6.1.a on page 302.

M.6.2.d   Does your workplace/placement have a policy on confidentiality of information? Make a list of its key points.

M.6.3 Work in co-operation with other professionals

	Criteria	Knowledge evidence	Date completed
PROGRESS CHECKLIST	M.6.3.a	The stereotypical assumptions which can be made in sharing out work.	
	M.6.3.b	The nature and limits of working relationships within the organisation.	
	M.6.3.c	The nature and characteristics of professionalism in this field.	

USEFUL BOOKS

Working with Children. D. Houghton and M. McColgan (1995) Collins Educational.
Communicating with Children and Adults: Interpersonal Skills for those Working with Babies and Children. P. Petrie (1989) Edward Arnold.
The Early Years: Laying the Foundations for Racial Equality. I. Sirjai-Blatchford (1994) Trentham Books.
53 Interesting Ways to Promote Equal Opportunities in Education. V. Lewis and S. Habeshaw (1990) Technical and Educational Services.
Effective Meeting Skills. M. Hayes (1988) Kogan Page.
How to Make Meetings Work. M. Peel (1989) Kogan Page.

PORTFOLIO ACTIVITY SUMMARY				
Criteria	Portfolio page reference	0–1	1–4	4–7
M.6.3.a	See page 305 for Portfolio Activity			
M.6.3.b	See page 307 for Portfolio Activity			

 ### M.6.3.a Portfolio Activity

See M.6.2.b on page 305.

M.6.3.b *Portfolio Activity*

Devise a role play scenario of a team meeting. Choose the team leader's style and decide on roles for the other members of the team which should include staff and other professionals connected with special needs. The team leader's style can be autocratic, democratic or laissez-faire. Discuss how the style affects the contributions made by the team.

M.6.3.c **Case 1:** Saleem is a three-year-old at nursery school. One day, when you are looking at his painting, he says, 'My mum shouted at my dad and she's gone away now.' How do you react? Do you report it to anyone or not? Should you, or a senior worker, 'check out' if what Saleem says is true? What are your reasons for your course of action?

Case 2: In a maternity unit a weeping mother is having problems feeding her new baby. She tells you that she suffered severe depression after the birth of her first baby. What do you do, if anything, about this information? Why?

Case 3: You are an officer-in-charge of a day nursery. Gary's mother tells you that his father has AIDS. To whom – if anyone – do you pass this information on to? On what grounds do you make this decision?

Case 4: You do a home visit to a family where the child has just started nursery class. Wayne's mother tells you, in confidence, that his father is beating him. What do you say to her and what action, if any, do you take?

Read the above case studies. Then decide what you would do in each situation. There may not be one 'right' answer; you may think of different circumstances which could affect what you would do.

(**Adapted from** Petrie, 1989; pp. 63–64.)

GLOSSARY

ailments   illnesses

'at risk'   the chance that the health or development of a person may be damaged by certain conditions or actions of others. Care professionals use the phrase 'at risk' to indicate that a client is exposed to some source of harm and that possibly some protective measures should be taken. For example, a 'child at risk' is regarded as vulnerable to physical or sexual abuse by one or more people, or to other sources of harm through parental neglect

carer   any person who is taking care of a child or a number of children

chronic medical condition   a lasting condition that requires the attention of a physician

communicable disease   a disease that can be transmitted from one person to another

dietary requirement   essential food (nutrients)

disclosure   when a child tells or otherwise represents that they have been sexually abused

halal   meat from animals killed in accordance with the religious beliefs of Muslims

implementation plan   ideas to be put into place by all staff while a policy is being prepared

locomotion   the nervous system produces the necessary movements to enable the child to walk. From sitting, crawling, standing to walking

mobility   freedom to move

non-stereotypical   not making assumptions based on a child's race or gender

nutritional requirements   *see* dietary requirements

paediatric   the branch of medicine dealing with childhood diseases

phobia   understood widely in the medical profession as *neuroses* and very closely linked to the condition of *anxiety*. Phobias can be further regarded as mental illness and thus the person with a phobia may be regarded and treated negatively in society because of this label

psychologist   a specialist in the scientific study of the mind

rationale   the primary reason for something

reinforcement   used in relation to behaviour whereby the carer/adult would support behaviour and strengthen acceptable behaviour

sanction   approval that is given to rules

sound discrimination   the ability to make distinctions of sound

spatial awareness   being conscious of space (room)

special needs child(ren)   a child or children whose condition makes them need a special kind of care and understanding

specialist   an expert in a subject. For example, a surgeon is an expert in performing operations

spidergram/topic web   a web of ideas based around a central theme

sterilised   free from germs

symptoms   a change in the body (noticed by patient or carer) indicating a disease or
    disorder
unconscious(ness)   being unaware of surroundings, or not responding to stimulation
weaning   reducing milk feeds and gradually introducing solid foods
workplan   a list of ideas to work through